Australia

Everything You Need to Know

Introduction

Australia, often referred to as the "Land Down Under," is a vast and diverse continent that captivates the imagination of travelers and enthusiasts from around the world. Situated in the Southern Hemisphere, Australia is not just a country; it's a unique blend of history, culture, and natural wonders that have evolved over millions of years.

One of the most defining features of Australia is its sheer size. It's the sixth-largest country in the world by land area, covering approximately 2.94 million square miles (7.66 million square kilometers). To put this into perspective, you could fit the entire continental United States within Australia and still have plenty of room to spare. This vast expanse of land means that Australia boasts a wide range of landscapes, climates, and ecosystems, from tropical rainforests to arid deserts.

One of Australia's most iconic natural wonders is the Great Barrier Reef, the world's largest coral reef system. Stretching over 1,400 miles (2,300 kilometers) along the northeastern coast, this UNESCO World Heritage site is renowned for its stunning marine biodiversity. It's a haven for divers and snorkelers, offering a glimpse into a vibrant underwater world filled with colorful corals, fish, and marine creatures.

Australia's diverse geography also includes the famous Outback, a vast arid region that covers much of the interior. Here, you'll find the expansive desert landscapes, such as the Simpson Desert and the Great Victoria Desert. The Outback is known for its rugged beauty, rich Aboriginal heritage, and the famous red sands of Uluru (Ayers Rock) and Kata Tjuta (the Olgas). Speaking of Aboriginal heritage, it's essential to acknowledge that Australia's history dates back tens of thousands of years, long before European settlement. Indigenous Australians, often referred to as Aboriginal and Torres Strait Islander peoples, have a deep connection to the land and hold a rich cultural heritage. Their traditions, languages, and Dreamtime stories are an integral part of Australia's identity.

Australia's European history began with the arrival of British convicts in 1788 when the First Fleet landed in what is now Sydney. The British established a penal colony in New South Wales, marking the start of European settlement on the continent. Over the years, more colonies were established, leading to the eventual federation of Australia as a nation in 1901.

Today, Australia is a thriving multicultural society, known for its friendly people, high quality of life, and vibrant cities. Sydney, the largest and most iconic city, is famous for its stunning harbor and landmarks like the Sydney Opera House and Sydney Harbour Bridge. Melbourne, on the other hand, is renowned for its arts and culture scene, while Brisbane offers a laid-back lifestyle and access to beautiful beaches.

As we delve deeper into this book, we will explore Australia's history, its unique wildlife, cuisine, and the essential aspects of its major cities. We will also dive into the cultural tapestry of this remarkable nation, including its art, music, and traditions. In addition, we will learn about the languages spoken in Australia and how they reflect its diverse population. So, join me on this journey as we unravel the wonders of Australia, the Land Down Under.

Australia's Indigenous History

Australia's Indigenous history is a narrative that stretches back tens of thousands of years, long before the arrival of European settlers on the continent's shores. It is a history deeply rooted in the connection between the Aboriginal and Torres Strait Islander peoples and the vast, diverse landscapes that make up this ancient land.

The Indigenous peoples of Australia are believed to have inhabited the continent for at least 65,000 years, making them one of the world's oldest continuous cultures. Their profound connection to the land is evident in their Dreamtime stories, which are foundational to their spiritual and cultural beliefs. These stories are a way of explaining the creation of the world, the land, and all living things. They are handed down through generations, preserving ancient wisdom and knowledge.

The Aboriginal peoples are not a single, homogenous group but rather a mosaic of hundreds of distinct nations, each with its languages, traditions, and territories. In contrast, the Torres Strait Islander peoples inhabit the islands between the northern tip of Queensland and Papua New Guinea, characterized by their unique cultures and languages.

These Indigenous communities have a deep respect for the environment and a sustainable way of life that has allowed them to thrive in some of the harshest conditions on Earth. They are skilled hunters and gatherers, using their knowledge of the land to find food, water, and shelter. Traditional practices such as fire management and land cultivation have shaped the Australian landscape over thousands of years. The arrival of European explorers in the late 18th century marked a significant turning point in Australia's Indigenous history. As British colonization advanced, it led to violent clashes, diseases, and the dispossession of Indigenous lands. The impact of these events is still felt today, as many Indigenous communities continue to grapple with the legacy of colonization.

One of the most tragic aspects of this history is the Stolen Generations, a period from the late 19th century to the mid-20th century when Indigenous children were forcibly removed from their families and communities. This policy aimed to assimilate Indigenous children into European culture and resulted in the traumatic separation of families and the loss of cultural heritage.

Throughout the 20th century, there were significant movements for Indigenous rights and recognition. In 1967, a referendum saw an overwhelming majority of Australians vote in favor of recognizing Indigenous people in the national census and giving the federal government the power to make laws specifically for their benefit.

In 2008, the Australian government issued a formal apology to the Stolen Generations, acknowledging the pain and suffering inflicted on Indigenous peoples. This apology marked a critical moment in the ongoing process of reconciliation and healing.

Today, Australia is committed to recognizing the rights and contributions of its Indigenous peoples. Efforts are being made to preserve and revive Indigenous languages, promote cultural education, and address the socioeconomic disparities that persist within Indigenous communities.

Early European Exploration

The story of early European exploration in Australia is a tale of bold voyages, uncharted territories, and the quest for new horizons. It's a narrative that begins in the late 16th century when European powers, primarily Spain, Portugal, and the Netherlands, were expanding their reach across the globe.

The first recorded European sighting of Australia is attributed to the Dutch navigator Willem Janszoon in 1606. Sailing aboard the Duyfken, Janszoon landed on the western coast of Cape York Peninsula, in what is now Queensland. This event marked the beginning of European interaction with the Australian continent.

Over the following decades, Dutch explorers like Dirk Hartog and Abel Tasman continued to chart parts of the Australian coastline. In 1616, Dirk Hartog left behind an inscribed pewter plate on the island that now bears his name, providing evidence of his landing.

In 1642, Abel Tasman, while searching for the fabled southern continent, encountered the island of Tasmania, which he named Van Diemen's Land after the governor of the Dutch East Indies. Tasman also charted parts of the western and northern coasts of Australia during his voyages.

The 17th century saw limited European exploration in the region, primarily driven by Dutch interests in trade and navigation. However, it was not until the late 18th century that European exploration in Australia would intensify, driven by British ambitions and the scientific curiosity of the era.

In 1768, the British Royal Navy commissioned Captain James Cook to undertake a voyage to the Pacific Ocean to observe the transit of Venus and search for the elusive southern continent. Cook's first voyage on the HMS Endeavour brought him to the eastern coast of Australia in 1770, where he made the first recorded European contact with the continent's eastern shores. Cook named the area New South Wales, claiming it for the British Crown.

Cook's voyage paved the way for further British exploration and eventual colonization. In 1788, the First Fleet, led by Captain Arthur Phillip, arrived in Botany Bay (now part of Sydney), establishing the first British penal colony in Australia. This event marked the beginning of European settlement on the continent.

Exploration efforts continued throughout the late 18th and early 19th centuries, as explorers like Matthew Flinders, George Bass, and John Oxley ventured inland and mapped various parts of the Australian coastline. These explorations were driven by a combination of scientific curiosity, a desire to chart the uncharted, and the need to find suitable areas for settlement.

European exploration of Australia was not without its challenges and hardships. Explorers faced treacherous terrain, harsh climates, and encounters with Indigenous peoples, which sometimes led to conflict. Yet, their efforts laid the foundation for the eventual colonization and development of Australia.

The First Fleet and Convict Settlement

The arrival of the First Fleet in 1788 marked a significant chapter in Australia's history, as it heralded the establishment of the first European settlement on the continent. This pivotal event was a culmination of British ambitions, penal reform, and the desire to expand British influence in the Pacific.

Under the command of Captain Arthur Phillip, the First Fleet consisted of 11 ships that set sail from England in May 1787, carrying around 1,500 people. Among the passengers were approximately 780 convicts, men and women who had been sentenced to transportation as a form of punishment for their crimes. The rest of the fleet comprised marines, officers, free settlers, and crew members.

The fleet's primary destination was Botany Bay, a location identified by Captain James Cook during his voyage in 1770. However, upon arrival in January 1788, Captain Phillip deemed Botany Bay unsuitable for settlement due to its lack of fresh water and poor soil quality. Instead, the fleet sailed a short distance north and anchored in Port Jackson, where they established the first European settlement in Australia, later to become Sydney.

Life in the early days of the settlement was incredibly challenging. The convicts and settlers faced the harsh Australian environment, including unfamiliar flora and fauna, as well as the formidable Australian summer heat. Freshwater was scarce, and food supplies were limited, leading to a struggle for survival. Disease, particularly scurvy, took a toll on the settlers.

To address these challenges, the settlement relied heavily on the skills of the convicts, who were tasked with clearing land, building shelters, and growing crops. The arrival of the Second Fleet in 1790 brought much-needed additional supplies and personnel, but it also brought with it further hardship, as the fleet's convicts were in poor health.

Despite the initial hardships, the settlement gradually began to stabilize and grow. Farming and agriculture improved, and the colony expanded beyond Sydney. The establishment of secondary convict settlements, such as Parramatta and Norfolk Island, helped relieve overcrowding and provide more opportunities for agriculture.

The convict labor force played a crucial role in the development of the colony. Many convicts served their sentences and were eventually granted pardons, allowing them to become free settlers. This transition from a penal colony to a free society marked a significant turning point in Australia's history.

As the colony grew, so did its interactions with the Indigenous peoples of the area, the Eora and Gadigal people, among others. These interactions were complex, ranging from friendly exchanges to conflicts over land and resources. The impact of European settlement on Indigenous communities was profound, leading to dispossession and significant disruptions to their traditional way of life.

The First Fleet and the early years of convict settlement laid the foundation for modern Australia. The struggles and resilience of those early settlers, both convicts and free settlers, contributed to the development of a unique Australian identity. Over time, the colony would expand, and new waves of immigrants would shape the nation, leading to the vibrant and diverse society that Australia is today.

Colonization and the Gold Rush

The period of colonization and the subsequent gold rush in Australia represents a pivotal era in the nation's history, characterized by rapid growth, profound social changes, and economic transformation. This chapter delves into the dynamic events that unfolded during this time, reshaping the continent and the lives of its inhabitants.

Following the establishment of the first European settlement in Sydney in 1788, British colonization expanded steadily throughout the 19th century. The British government saw Australia as a strategic outpost, a place to send convicts, and eventually, a destination for free settlers seeking new opportunities. As the colony grew, so did the demand for land, resources, and labor.

In the early 1800s, explorers like John Hume and Hamilton Hume ventured into the interior, opening up new regions for settlement. The fertile lands of New South Wales attracted both free settlers and emancipated convicts eager to acquire property and establish farms.

The expansion of colonization was not without conflict. As Europeans pushed further into Indigenous lands, clashes between settlers and Indigenous communities became more frequent. The dispossession of land and resources had devastating consequences for Indigenous peoples, leading to displacement and profound social disruption.

The 19th century brought significant developments to the Australian colonies. The transportation of convicts continued until 1868 when the last ship carrying convicts arrived in Western Australia. By this time, the colonies had begun to evolve into self-governing entities, each with its own parliament and laws. It was during this period that gold was discovered in several Australian colonies, setting off a series of gold rushes that would change the course of the nation's history. The first significant discovery was made in 1851 in New South Wales, sparking the Australian gold rush. Thousands of prospectors flocked to the goldfields, hoping to strike it rich.

Victoria soon became the epicenter of the gold rush, particularly with the discovery of gold in Ballarat and Bendigo. This led to a massive influx of fortune seekers from around the world, creating a diverse and dynamic population. The Eureka Stockade in Ballarat in 1854 stands as a symbol of the struggle for miners' rights during this time.

The gold rushes had profound economic and social impacts. They stimulated the development of infrastructure, including roads, railways, and towns. Melbourne, in particular, experienced rapid growth and became one of the wealthiest and most populous cities in the British Empire during this period.

The gold rushes also played a role in shaping Australia's identity. The influx of immigrants from various backgrounds contributed to the nation's multicultural fabric. Additionally, the demands of the goldfields led to innovations in mining technology and practices, which would benefit other industries in the years to come.

While the gold rushes brought prosperity to many, they also created significant disparities. The wealth generated from gold mining was not equally distributed, and the living conditions for many miners were harsh and dangerous. This period also saw the emergence of labor movements advocating for workers' rights and better working conditions.

Federation and the Birth of a Nation

The journey towards the federation of Australia was a complex and transformative process that ultimately led to the birth of a nation. This chapter explores the pivotal events and key figures that played significant roles in shaping the federation of Australia as we know it today.

By the late 19th century, the various Australian colonies had developed their governments, each with its own set of laws and regulations. However, there was growing recognition of the need for a unified nation that could coordinate matters of national interest, such as defense and trade, while still preserving regional autonomy.

One of the key milestones in the path to federation was the drafting of the Australian Constitution. This document, largely influenced by the United States Constitution, outlined the framework for a federal government that would oversee the nation's affairs. The Constitution was drafted through a series of conventions held in the 1890s.

In 1901, the Australian Constitution came into effect when six of the colonies—New South Wales, Victoria, Queensland, South Australia, Western Australia, and Tasmania—voted to federate and form the Commonwealth of Australia. The capital city was established in Canberra, chosen as a compromise between the competing claims of Sydney and Melbourne.

The formation of the Commonwealth of Australia also marked the birth of a new federal government with its own parliament, executive branch, and legal system. Sir

Edmund Barton, a prominent lawyer and politician, became the nation's first Prime Minister, overseeing this critical period of transition. The federation process was not without challenges. It required careful negotiation and compromise among the colonies, each of which had its own interests and concerns. These negotiations culminated in the drafting of the Constitution, which was approved through referendums in the colonies.

The inclusion of the term "White Australia Policy" in the Constitution reflected the prevailing attitudes of the time. This policy aimed to restrict non-European immigration and maintain a predominantly Anglo-Saxon population in Australia. It had significant implications for immigration and Indigenous rights, and it remained in effect until after World War II. With the federation came a sense of national identity and pride. The new nation sought to define itself on the world stage, and Australia's participation in the First World War in 1914 was a significant moment that reinforced its ties with the British Empire and the global community.

The years following federation saw the establishment of key institutions and policies that shaped modern Australia. The Commonwealth Bank was founded in 1911, and a national currency was introduced. Social policies, such as the introduction of a maternity allowance and old-age pensions, improved the welfare of citizens.

The Anzac legend, born from the heroism and sacrifice of Australian and New Zealand soldiers during World War I, further strengthened the sense of national identity and camaraderie among Australians. The legacy of Anzac Day, commemorated on April 25th each year, continues to be an integral part of Australian culture.

World Wars and Australia's Role

The world wars of the 20th century had a profound impact on Australia and its place in the global arena. As a young nation, Australia found itself thrust into the center of these global conflicts, playing a crucial role in both World War I and World War II.

World War I, which erupted in 1914, marked Australia's first major involvement in a global conflict as a federated nation. When Britain declared war on Germany, Australia, as part of the British Empire, also entered the conflict. Thousands of young Australians answered the call to serve, and the Australian Imperial Force (AIF) was formed. They became known as the Anzacs, and their bravery and sacrifice on the battlefields of Gallipoli, the Western Front, and other theaters of war left an indelible mark on the nation's psyche.

The Gallipoli Campaign of 1915, in particular, holds a special place in Australian history. The Anzacs faced incredibly challenging conditions, including fierce battles, harsh terrain, and the threat of disease. Despite the campaign's ultimate failure, it became a symbol of Australian resilience and mateship, and April 25th, now known as Anzac Day, is commemorated nationwide to honor their sacrifice.

Australia's participation in World War I extended beyond Gallipoli. The AIF fought on the Western Front, where they played a significant role in battles such as Fromelles, Pozieres, and Villers-Bretonneux. By the end of the war,

Australia had suffered substantial casualties, with over 60,000 lives lost and many more wounded.

World War I also had far-reaching consequences for the nation's identity and politics. The war experience fostered a greater sense of national pride and a growing desire for greater independence from Britain. This sentiment contributed to the development of a distinct Australian identity and the eventual Statute of Westminster in 1931, which granted Australia legislative independence from the British Parliament.

Following the end of World War I, Australia entered a period of recovery and reconstruction, but the world was soon plunged into another devastating conflict, World War II, in 1939. Once again, Australia committed its forces to support Britain, this time against Nazi Germany and its allies.

The war had a profound impact on Australia's homefront. The threat of Japanese invasion in the Pacific led to the deployment of Australian troops to defend Papua New Guinea and other strategic locations. The bombing of Darwin in 1942 was a stark reminder of the war's proximity to Australian shores.

The Australian people, both at home and abroad, made significant sacrifices during World War II. The conflict saw increased industrialization and economic growth, with women playing a vital role in the workforce. Rationing and wartime restrictions affected daily life, as the nation rallied to support the war effort.

Australian forces fought in various theaters of World War II, including North Africa, the Mediterranean, and the

Pacific. The Battle of Kokoda in Papua New Guinea, where Australian troops played a pivotal role in halting the Japanese advance, is remembered as a defining moment of the conflict.

After the war, Australia played a role in the establishment of the United Nations and participated in post-war reconstruction efforts. The war also prompted a wave of immigration, with displaced persons and war brides contributing to the nation's growing cultural diversity.

Modern Australia: A Multicultural Nation

Modern Australia is a vibrant and diverse nation, characterized by its rich multicultural tapestry. The story of Australia's journey to becoming a multicultural society is a fascinating one, marked by waves of immigration, social changes, and a commitment to inclusivity.

Australia's multicultural journey can be traced back to the mid-20th century when the government initiated policies to encourage immigration from countries beyond the traditional British sources. This shift was partly driven by the recognition that Australia needed to increase its population and workforce for economic growth and development.

One of the significant milestones in Australia's multicultural history was the Immigration Restriction Act of 1901, which introduced the infamous White Australia Policy, aiming to restrict immigration to those of European descent. However, following World War II, this policy gradually gave way to a more inclusive approach.

In the aftermath of the war, Australia welcomed waves of immigrants from Europe, including displaced persons and refugees. These newcomers brought with them diverse cultural backgrounds, languages, and traditions. They settled in various parts of Australia, contributing to the nation's cultural mosaic.

The 1950s and 1960s saw further changes in immigration policy, including the abolition of the White Australia Policy and the implementation of more open and inclusive policies. As a result, people from a wide range of countries, including Italy, Greece, Yugoslavia, and later, Southeast Asian nations, began to make Australia their home.

One of the most significant turning points in Australia's multicultural history was the decision to grant equal rights and citizenship to Indigenous Australians in 1967. This constitutional change marked a commitment to recognizing the rights and contributions of the nation's First Peoples, although it would take many more years to address the ongoing disparities faced by Indigenous communities.

The 1970s and 1980s witnessed a further diversification of Australia's immigrant population, with an influx of people from Asia, the Middle East, and Africa. This era saw the development of multicultural policies aimed at fostering inclusivity, respecting cultural diversity, and promoting social cohesion.

Australia's multiculturalism is enshrined in its policies and institutions. The establishment of bodies such as the Special Broadcasting Service (SBS) and the Australian Multicultural Foundation reflects the government's commitment to promoting diversity and intercultural understanding. These institutions have played a vital role in celebrating cultural diversity through media, education, and community programs.

The multicultural fabric of Australia is reflected in its cities, where you can find neighborhoods and precincts dedicated to specific cultural communities. Sydney's Chinatown, Melbourne's Little Italy, and the multicultural suburb of Lakemba in Sydney are just a few examples of the vibrant cultural enclaves that exist across the nation.

Today, Australia is proud of its multicultural identity. The nation celebrates cultural festivals and events, embraces diverse cuisines, and values the contributions of immigrants to the country's social, economic, and cultural life. This diversity has enriched Australia's art, music, food, and language, making it a truly global and inclusive society.

Australia's multicultural journey is an ongoing story, one that continues to evolve as new waves of immigrants arrive from all corners of the world. The nation's commitment to multiculturalism serves as a source of strength and unity, reflecting the belief that diversity is not only to be embraced but celebrated as an integral part of what it means to be Australian in the modern era.

Australia's Unique Geography and Climate

Australia, often referred to as the "Land Down Under," boasts some of the world's most distinctive and diverse geographical and climatic features. Its vast expanse encompasses a wide range of landscapes, climates, and natural wonders, making it a land like no other.

One of Australia's most defining geographical features is its sheer size. It is the sixth-largest country in the world by land area, covering approximately 2.94 million square miles (7.66 million square kilometers). To put this into perspective, you could fit the entire continental United States within Australia and still have plenty of room to spare.

The continent is surrounded by water, with the Indian Ocean to the west, the Pacific Ocean to the east, and the Southern Ocean to the south. The northern coast is fringed with the Timor Sea, Arafura Sea, and the Coral Sea, making it a land girt by sea on all sides.

Australia's vast interior is dominated by the Outback, a vast arid region that covers much of the continent. Here, you'll find iconic features like the red sands of Uluru (Ayers Rock) and Kata Tjuta (the Olgas), which rise from the desert floor. The Outback is known for its rugged beauty, rich Aboriginal heritage, and unique flora and fauna adapted to harsh conditions.

The eastern part of Australia is home to the Great Dividing Range, a mountain range that stretches over 2,300 miles (3,700 kilometers) and influences much of the country's weather patterns. The eastern slopes of this range are lush and green, with fertile valleys and rainforests, while the western slopes give way to arid plains.

Australia's coastline is exceptionally varied, with long stretches of sandy beaches, rugged cliffs, and diverse ecosystems. The Great Barrier Reef, located off the northeastern coast, is the world's largest coral reef system and a UNESCO World Heritage site. It's renowned for its stunning marine biodiversity, attracting divers and snorkelers from around the globe.

The continent's climate is equally diverse, thanks to its vast size and geographical variations. Australia experiences a range of climate zones, from tropical in the north to arid and semi-arid in the interior, temperate along the southern coast, and even alpine in the southeast.

The north of Australia is characterized by a tropical climate with distinct wet and dry seasons. It experiences heavy rainfall during the monsoon season, which can lead to flooding in some areas. The south, on the other hand, has four distinct seasons, with mild winters and warm summers.

The central regions of Australia are known for their extreme temperatures, with scorching summers and cold winters. In places like Alice Springs, temperatures can soar above 100°F (37°C) during the day and drop significantly at night.

Australia's unique geographical features and climate have had a profound influence on its ecosystems and wildlife. The continent is home to a remarkable array of native species, many of which are found nowhere else on Earth. From iconic marsupials like kangaroos and koalas to the elusive platypus and the deadly saltwater crocodile, Australia's wildlife is both diverse and unique.

In conclusion, Australia's unique geography and climate have shaped the nation's identity and way of life. Its vast landscapes, coastal wonders, and climatic variations have given rise to a rich tapestry of ecosystems and habitats, making it a land of remarkable natural beauty and ecological significance. It is a place where the extraordinary thrives, and its geographical and climatic diversity is a testament to the wonders of the Land Down Under.

The Great Barrier Reef: World's Largest Coral Reef System

The Great Barrier Reef, a natural wonder of unparalleled beauty and ecological significance, is the world's largest coral reef system. Located off the northeastern coast of Australia, this stunning marine ecosystem stretches over 1,400 miles (2,300 kilometers) and covers an area of approximately 133,000 square miles (344,400 square kilometers). It's so vast that it can be seen from space, earning its reputation as one of the Seven Natural Wonders of the World.

This remarkable reef system is composed of over 2,900 individual reefs and 900 islands, creating a complex and intricate underwater world. The reef is a biodiversity hotspot, home to an astonishing array of marine life, including thousands of species of fish, coral, mollusks, sea turtles, sharks, and marine mammals.

At the heart of the Great Barrier Reef is its stunning coral formations, which are primarily made up of hard corals known as scleractinians. These corals provide the structural framework for the entire ecosystem. Over time, layers of coral polyps build upon one another, creating the intricate structures we see today. The reef's vibrant and diverse corals come in a kaleidoscope of colors, from brilliant blues and purples to vivid oranges and greens. The Great Barrier Reef is not just a natural wonder; it's also an ecological powerhouse. It supports a staggering diversity of life, with more than 1,500 species of fish alone. It serves as a crucial breeding ground for numerous marine species, including several species of sea turtles that lay their eggs on its sandy cays. One of the most iconic inhabitants of the reef is the charismatic clownfish, made famous by the animated film "Finding Nemo." These small, colorful fish live among the stinging tentacles of sea anemones and have a fascinating symbiotic relationship with these creatures. The clownfish are immune to the anemone's sting and provide food for them in return.

The reef also hosts a variety of shark species, including the graceful reef shark and the formidable hammerhead shark. While the Great Barrier Reef is home to some shark species, it is not a hotspot for large, dangerous sharks. Instead, it's a sanctuary for numerous species of smaller sharks and rays.

The Great Barrier Reef is a UNESCO World Heritage site and is recognized for its outstanding universal value and significance. It plays a vital role in the global ecosystem, as coral reefs like this one support a quarter of all marine species, despite covering less than 0.1% of the ocean floor.

However, the reef faces significant challenges, primarily due to climate change, which has led to rising sea temperatures and ocean acidification. These environmental stressors have resulted in coral bleaching events, where corals expel the symbiotic algae that provide them with food and color. Bleached corals are more vulnerable to disease and death, posing a threat to the entire ecosystem.

Efforts are underway to protect and preserve the Great Barrier Reef. Conservation initiatives, sustainable tourism practices, and research programs aim to better understand and mitigate the impacts of climate change and human activity on this fragile ecosystem.

Australia's Diverse Wildlife

Australia is renowned for its extraordinary and diverse wildlife, with a unique array of creatures that have evolved in isolation on this ancient continent. From iconic marsupials to remarkable reptiles and captivating birdlife, Australia's ecosystems teem with life found nowhere else on Earth.

Perhaps one of the first images that come to mind when thinking of Australian wildlife is the kangaroo. These marsupials are quintessentially Australian, known for their powerful hind legs and distinctive hopping gait. There are several species of kangaroos, including the red kangaroo, the largest marsupial on the planet, and the smaller, more agile wallabies. Kangaroos are herbivores and are adapted to the arid landscapes of the Outback.

Another marsupial that captivates visitors and locals alike is the koala. These tree-dwelling mammals are often referred to as "koala bears" due to their bear-like appearance, but they are not bears at all. Koalas are arboreal herbivores, primarily feeding on eucalyptus leaves. They are known for their cuddly appearance and are a symbol of Australian wildlife.

Australia's marsupials also include the iconic wombat, known for its burrowing habits and sturdy build, and the Tasmanian devil, a carnivorous marsupial found only in Tasmania. The Tasmanian devil is known for its ferocious demeanor and loud, guttural calls.

Moving to the realm of monotremes, Australia is home to two unique egg-laying mammals: the platypus and the echidna. The platypus, often described as a "duck-billed" mammal, is known for its bizarre combination of features, including webbed feet, a bill, and the ability to lay eggs. Echidnas, on the other hand, have spiky quills and long, sticky tongues used to capture ants and termites, their primary food source.

Australia's birdlife is equally fascinating, with species ranging from the colorful rainbow lorikeet to the majestic wedge-tailed eagle. The emu, Australia's largest bird and second-largest in the world, is known for its flightless nature and distinctive appearance. Emus are found throughout Australia and are an integral part of Indigenous culture.

Australia's reptilian inhabitants are no less remarkable. The saltwater crocodile, one of the world's largest reptiles, is found in northern Australian waters. It's known for its immense size and formidable predatory abilities. On the other end of the scale, the frilled-neck lizard is a striking reptile with a frill of skin around its neck, used for intimidation displays.

Australia's seas are home to an array of marine life, including the dugong, a large marine mammal known as the "sea cow," and the vibrant clownfish, made famous by the film "Finding Nemo." The Great Barrier Reef, one of the Seven Natural Wonders of the World, shelters a dazzling array of coral species and marine creatures, from colorful parrotfish to graceful manta rays.

Unique to Australia is the presence of marsupial carnivores, known as dasyurids, which include the Tasmanian tiger (thylacine) and the Tasmanian devil. Unfortunately, the thylacine is believed to be extinct, but the Tasmanian devil still roams the wilds of Tasmania.

Australia's diverse wildlife also includes a host of insects, spiders, and amphibians, many of which are still being discovered and studied by scientists. The continent's unique ecosystems, from rainforests to deserts, provide a wide range of habitats for these fascinating creatures.

Conservation efforts are essential to protect Australia's diverse wildlife, as many species are threatened by habitat loss, climate change, and introduced predators. Organizations and researchers are working diligently to ensure the survival of these unique and irreplaceable species.

Exploring the Australian Outback

The Australian Outback, often referred to as the "Red Center," is a vast and remote region that stretches across the heart of the continent. It's a place of stark beauty, extreme landscapes, and a sense of isolation that is unlike anywhere else in the world. This chapter delves into the mystique and allure of the Outback, a place where adventurers and nature enthusiasts seek to experience the raw essence of Australia.

One of the first things that strike visitors to the Outback is its sheer vastness. It covers approximately 70% of the Australian continent, and its landscapes vary from arid deserts to rugged mountain ranges. The iconic red soil, which gives the Outback its nickname, is a result of the iron-rich earth oxidizing over millions of years.

Uluru, also known as Ayers Rock, is perhaps the most famous symbol of the Outback. This massive sandstone monolith rises dramatically from the flat desert landscape, changing colors throughout the day as the sun moves across the sky. It holds immense cultural and spiritual significance for Indigenous Australians, and visitors come from around the world to witness its majesty.

Kata Tjuta, or the Olgas, is another remarkable geological formation in the region. This series of domed rock formations, located not far from Uluru, is equally captivating and sacred to the Anangu people.

The Outback is known for its extreme temperatures, with scorching summers and chilly winters. In places like

Birdsville and Oodnadatta, temperatures can soar above 110°F (43°C) during the day, while at night, they can plummet to near freezing. The climate is harsh, and water is often scarce, making survival a daily challenge for both wildlife and humans.

Despite the seemingly inhospitable conditions, the Outback is teeming with life. Unique flora and fauna have adapted to the arid environment, including hardy eucalyptus trees, spinifex grasses, and resilient desert plants. Wildlife such as kangaroos, wallabies, emus, and wedge-tailed eagles call this harsh terrain home.

One of the joys of exploring the Outback is encountering its Indigenous culture and history. Indigenous Australians have a deep connection to this land that spans tens of thousands of years. Their knowledge of the land's resources and survival skills in the Outback are awe-inspiring.

To venture into the Outback is to embark on an adventure of a lifetime. It's a place where you can travel for days without seeing another soul, where the night skies are ablaze with stars, and where the silence is broken only by the sound of the wind and the calls of nocturnal creatures.

Many travelers explore the Outback by taking on iconic road trips, like the Stuart Highway, which crosses the continent from north to south, or the Gibb River Road in Western Australia, known for its rugged terrain and stunning gorges. Four-wheel drive vehicles are often essential for navigating the rough tracks and river crossings.

For those seeking an even more remote experience, there are guided tours and safari expeditions that offer a glimpse into the Outback's hidden corners. These journeys provide the opportunity to learn about the region's natural history, Indigenous culture, and the challenges of surviving in this unforgiving environment.

The Australian Outback is a land of contrasts, where solitude and isolation are balanced by the beauty of its landscapes and the warmth of its people. It's a place where the ancient meets the modern, and where the spirit of adventure and exploration continues to thrive. To explore the Australian Outback is to step into the heart and soul of this vast and remarkable continent, where the journey itself is as meaningful as the destination.

Australian Cuisine: From Vegemite to Tim Tams

Australian cuisine is a reflection of the country's diverse culture, unique geography, and historical influences. While it may not have the international recognition of some other cuisines, it has its own distinctive flavors and iconic dishes that are cherished by Australians and gaining recognition worldwide.

One of the defining features of Australian cuisine is its fusion of culinary traditions from around the world. Australia's history of immigration has brought a wide variety of influences to its food. Indigenous Australian cuisine, with its focus on native ingredients like kangaroo, emu, and bush tucker, is an essential part of the country's food heritage.

Australia's colonial history also plays a significant role in its cuisine. British settlers brought with them traditional dishes such as roast meats, pies, and puddings, which remain popular today. The Sunday roast, featuring roasted meat, potatoes, and vegetables, is a beloved tradition.

Seafood is a prominent part of Australian cuisine, given the country's extensive coastline. Barramundi, prawns, oysters, and fish and chips are staples enjoyed by many Australians. Sydney's seafood markets are renowned for their fresh catches.

Australia's multiculturalism is reflected in its diverse range of foods. Italian, Greek, Chinese, Vietnamese, Lebanese, and Thai cuisines, among others, have all made their mark. Australian-Chinese dishes like sweet and sour pork and honey chicken are common in local Chinese restaurants.

One iconic Australian food item that often sparks curiosity among visitors is Vegemite. This dark, savory spread is made from leftover brewers' yeast extract and is typically spread thinly on buttered toast. While it's an acquired taste, many Australians grew up with it and consider it a national staple.

Tim Tams are another beloved Australian treat. These chocolate-coated biscuits, known for their indulgent flavors, are a favorite for dunking into a cup of tea or coffee. They come in various flavors, from classic chocolate to caramel and even mango.

Meat pies are a quintessential Australian fast food. These handheld pastries filled with minced meat and gravy are often enjoyed at sporting events. Sausage rolls, made with spiced sausage meat encased in flaky pastry, are another popular savory snack.

The barbecue, or "barbie" as it's affectionately called, is a central part of Australian outdoor culture. Australians love to grill meats and seafood, often in the great outdoors, taking advantage of the country's favorable climate.

Bush tucker, which includes native foods like quandong, wattleseed, and Kakadu plums, has gained recognition in recent years. These ingredients are being incorporated into modern Australian cuisine by innovative chefs and food producers.

Australia's wine regions, including the Barossa Valley and Margaret River, produce world-class wines. Shiraz, Chardonnay, and Sauvignon Blanc are just a few of the varieties enjoyed locally and exported worldwide.

Craft beer and artisanal spirits are also on the rise, with breweries and distilleries popping up across the country. Australians have embraced the craft beer movement, creating unique and flavorful brews.

In recent years, there has been a growing interest in sustainable and locally sourced ingredients, reflecting a broader global food trend. Farm-to-table restaurants and farmers' markets are flourishing, emphasizing the importance of fresh, seasonal produce.

In conclusion, Australian cuisine is a vibrant blend of flavors, influenced by Indigenous traditions, European heritage, and the multicultural fabric of the nation. From the humble Vegemite sandwich to gourmet dining experiences, Australian food culture continues to evolve and surprise, offering a rich and diverse culinary journey for those willing to explore it.

Iconic Australian Dishes and Beverages

Australian cuisine is a delightful blend of flavors, and some dishes and beverages have become icons that are synonymous with the Land Down Under. These culinary creations not only satisfy the taste buds but also tell a story of Australia's cultural heritage and its unique relationship with food.

1. **Vegemite:** Perhaps the most polarizing of all Australian foods, Vegemite is a thick, dark, salty spread made from brewers' yeast extract. Australians have a deep affection for it, and it's often spread thinly on buttered toast for breakfast or in a sandwich. It's an acquired taste, and while some find it too salty, many Australians can't start their day without it.
2. **Tim Tams:** These chocolate-coated biscuits have achieved legendary status in Australia. Tim Tams come in various flavors, from classic chocolate to caramel and even more exotic ones. They are the go-to treat for indulgence and are often enjoyed with a hot cup of tea or coffee.
3. **Lamingtons:** These square sponge cakes are dipped in chocolate icing and then coated in desiccated coconut. They are a beloved sweet treat often found at bake sales, celebrations, and morning teas.
4. **Meat Pies:** A true Australian classic, meat pies are savory pastries filled with minced meat and gravy, often enjoyed with tomato sauce (ketchup). They

are a staple of Australian fast food and are commonly consumed at sporting events.

5. **Sausage Rolls:** Similar to meat pies but in a different form, sausage rolls consist of spiced sausage meat encased in flaky pastry. They are a popular snack and party food.

6. **Barramundi:** As a delicious and versatile fish, barramundi is a favorite in Australian cuisine. It can be grilled, fried, or steamed and is often served with a squeeze of lemon and a side of vegetables.

7. **Damper:** Damper is a traditional bushman's bread, typically made with just flour, water, and a pinch of salt. It's often cooked over a campfire and served with golden syrup or jam.

8. **Pavlova:** A dessert that's the subject of friendly rivalry between Australia and New Zealand, pavlova is a meringue-based treat topped with whipped cream and fresh fruit. It's named after the famous Russian ballerina Anna Pavlova, who visited both countries in the 1920s.

9. **Anzac Biscuits:** These oat-based cookies have a special place in Australian hearts. They were originally created during World War I and sent to soldiers overseas. Today, they are enjoyed year-round but are especially popular on Anzac Day, a national day of remembrance.

10. **Flat White:** When it comes to coffee, Australians take their brew seriously. The flat white is a popular coffee choice, made with espresso and steamed milk. It's less frothy than a cappuccino and has a smooth, velvety texture.

11. **Australian Wine:** Australia is known for its excellent wine production. Regions like the Barossa Valley and Margaret River produce world-class

Shiraz, Chardonnay, and Sauvignon Blanc, among others.

12. **Bundaberg Ginger Beer:** This non-alcoholic beverage is famous for its spicy ginger flavor and is often enjoyed on a hot day. It's also a key ingredient in the classic Australian cocktail, the "Dark and Stormy."

These iconic Australian dishes and beverages showcase the country's culinary diversity and cultural heritage. From Vegemite to lamingtons, each item has a unique place in the hearts and palates of Australians, and they continue to be enjoyed by locals and curious visitors alike.

Sydney: Australia's Largest and Most Iconic City

Sydney, often regarded as the gateway to Australia, is the nation's largest and most iconic city. It's a place where natural beauty meets urban vibrancy, and where modern skyscrapers stand in harmony with the stunning landscapes that surround it. Sydney is not just a city; it's an experience, a lifestyle, and a destination that captures the essence of Australia.

Situated on the east coast of the continent, Sydney is known for its breathtaking harbor, which is dominated by the iconic Sydney Opera House and the Sydney Harbour Bridge. The harbor is a bustling hub of activity, where ferries transport commuters and visitors, and where sailboats and yachts glide gracefully across the shimmering waters.

The Sydney Opera House, with its distinctive sail-like architecture, is one of the most recognized and celebrated performing arts venues in the world. It hosts a wide range of performances, from opera and ballet to theater and music concerts. Its presence on Bennelong Point is not only an architectural marvel but also a symbol of Sydney's cultural richness.

The Sydney Harbour Bridge, affectionately known as the "Coathanger" due to its distinctive shape, is both a practical transport link and an engineering marvel. Visitors can climb to the top of the bridge for panoramic views of the city, an experience that offers a unique perspective on Sydney's skyline.

Sydney's city center is a bustling metropolis of skyscrapers, shopping precincts, and a thriving business district. The Central Business District (CBD) is where commerce, culture, and cuisine converge. It's home to renowned landmarks like the Queen Victoria Building, a historic shopping center, and Circular Quay, a waterfront area teeming with restaurants, cafes, and cultural attractions.

Sydney's urban fabric is complemented by its beautiful beaches, which are an integral part of the city's lifestyle. Bondi Beach, with its golden sands and vibrant surf culture, is world-famous and attracts sunseekers and surfers from all corners of the globe. Manly Beach, on the other side of the harbor, offers a relaxed coastal atmosphere and is easily accessible by ferry.

Beyond the city's immediate attractions, Sydney is surrounded by natural wonders. The Blue Mountains, located just a short drive from the city, are a World Heritage-listed region known for their dramatic landscapes, including deep valleys, rugged cliffs, and lush eucalyptus forests. The Three Sisters rock formation is a prominent highlight.

To the north, the Hunter Valley is Australia's oldest wine region, famous for its vineyards and cellar doors offering world-class wines. It's a popular destination for wine enthusiasts and food lovers.

Sydney's multiculturalism is reflected in its vibrant food scene. From fresh seafood at the Sydney Fish Market to international cuisine in the suburbs, the city offers a diverse range of culinary experiences. The Rocks, a historic area near Circular Quay, is known for its pubs, restaurants, and artisan markets.

Sydney's climate is characterized by warm summers and mild winters, making it an attractive destination year-round. The city hosts numerous festivals and events, including the spectacular New Year's Eve fireworks over Sydney Harbour.

With its blend of natural beauty, cultural richness, and cosmopolitan allure, Sydney embodies the essence of Australia's coastal urban lifestyle. It's a city where the old and the new coexist, where natural wonders are intertwined with urban sophistication, and where the spirit of exploration and discovery thrives. Sydney is not just a city; it's an enduring symbol of Australia's vibrant spirit and enduring allure.

Melbourne: A Cultural Hub

Melbourne, often referred to as Australia's cultural capital, is a city that pulsates with artistic vibrancy, culinary creativity, and a deep appreciation for all things cultural. It's a place where creativity knows no bounds and where the pursuit of the arts is a way of life. Melbourne's rich tapestry of culture weaves together a compelling narrative that has captivated both residents and visitors for generations.

Nestled in the southeastern state of Victoria, Melbourne is known for its eclectic neighborhoods, each with its own unique character. The city's Central Business District (CBD) boasts a skyline adorned with modern skyscrapers, but it's the laneways and hidden alleys that truly define Melbourne's character. These narrow passageways are lined with street art, cafes, boutique shops, and a constant buzz of activity.

Fitzroy, with its bohemian spirit, is a melting pot of artistic expression. Here, you'll find galleries showcasing contemporary art, independent theaters, and a thriving live music scene. Brunswick Street, the area's main thoroughfare, is a hub for alternative fashion and unique dining experiences.

South Yarra and Prahran are chic, upscale neighborhoods known for their boutique shopping and elegant dining. The Chapel Street precinct is famous for its fashion boutiques and stylish cafes, making it a popular destination for the fashion-conscious.

St. Kilda, with its beachside allure, offers a relaxed coastal atmosphere just a stone's throw from the CBD. It's home to the historic Luna Park amusement park and the iconic St. Kilda Pier, where little penguins return to their nests at sunset, delighting visitors.

Melbourne's cultural heart beats strongly in the arts precinct along the Yarra River. Here, you'll find the National Gallery of Victoria (NGV), Australia's oldest and most visited art museum, housing an extensive collection of Australian and international art. The Arts Centre Melbourne is a hub for performing arts, hosting everything from ballet and opera to contemporary theater.

The Melbourne Museum, situated in Carlton Gardens, explores the city's history, culture, and natural world. The Royal Exhibition Building, an architectural gem and UNESCO World Heritage site, stands adjacent to the museum.

Sport is a significant part of Melbourne's culture, and the city is known for its passionate love of Australian rules football, cricket, and tennis. The Melbourne Cricket Ground (MCG), often referred to as the "G," is a hallowed ground for sports enthusiasts and has a capacity that rivals some of the world's largest stadiums.

Melbourne's dining scene is a culinary adventure. The city's cultural diversity is reflected in its food, from Italian pasta in Lygon Street to authentic Asian flavors in Richmond and Footscray. The Queen Victoria Market is a food lover's paradise, offering fresh produce, gourmet delights, and an array of international cuisines.

Coffee culture is an art form in Melbourne, and the city boasts a thriving cafe scene. Locals take their coffee seriously, and baristas are considered artisans in their craft. The laneway cafes and hole-in-the-wall espresso bars offer a coffee experience like no other.

Melbourne's commitment to cultural events is evident in its calendar, which is packed with festivals and exhibitions. The Melbourne International Comedy Festival, Melbourne Fashion Festival, and Melbourne International Film Festival are just a few examples of the city's annual celebrations of art and culture.

In conclusion, Melbourne is a city that celebrates culture in all its forms. Its neighborhoods are canvases for creativity, its cultural institutions are world-class, and its culinary scene is a testament to diversity. Melbourne's culture is not confined to museums and galleries; it's woven into the very fabric of the city, creating an environment where innovation and expression thrive. It's a place where the arts are embraced, where coffee is savored, and where the pursuit of culture is a way of life. Melbourne is, without a doubt, a cultural hub that continues to inspire and enchant all who experience its vibrant spirit.

Brisbane: The Sunshine State's Capital

Brisbane, the capital of Queensland and affectionately known as the "Sunshine State's Capital," is a city that exudes warmth, both in its climate and its friendly atmosphere. Situated on the eastern coast of Australia, along the banks of the winding Brisbane River, this city is a dynamic blend of modernity and natural beauty.

The Brisbane River is not just a geographical feature; it's a defining element of the city's character. The river meanders through Brisbane's heart, creating a scenic backdrop for the urban landscape. The South Bank Parklands, with its lush gardens and man-made beach, provide a tranquil oasis along the river's edge, perfect for relaxation and recreation.

South Bank is also home to the Queensland Cultural Centre, a hub of arts and entertainment. Here, you'll find the Queensland Art Gallery, the Gallery of Modern Art (GOMA), and the Queensland Performing Arts Centre (QPAC). These institutions collectively celebrate the arts and culture, hosting exhibitions, performances, and festivals throughout the year.

The city's skyline is a testament to its growth and prosperity. Modern skyscrapers dot the horizon, reflecting Brisbane's status as a major economic and business hub in Australia. The Central Business District (CBD) is where commerce thrives, with bustling streets filled with workers, shoppers, and diners.

One of the iconic landmarks of Brisbane is the Story Bridge, an impressive steel cantilever bridge that spans the river. It's not only a vital transportation link but also a symbol of the city's resilience and innovation.

For those who appreciate history and heritage, Brisbane offers glimpses of its past through colonial-era architecture. The Old Windmill and Commissariat Store, both heritage-listed buildings, provide insights into the city's history.

Brisbane is a city of parks and green spaces, offering residents and visitors ample opportunities to enjoy the outdoors. The City Botanic Gardens, established in 1828, provide a serene escape from the urban hustle and bustle. The Roma Street Parkland, with its colorful flower beds and walking paths, is another popular green retreat.

Kangaroo Point Cliffs, rising dramatically from the river, offer stunning panoramic views of the city skyline and are a favorite spot for rock climbing and abseiling. The cliffs also provide the perfect backdrop for evening picnics and barbecues.

Brisbane's climate is subtropical, with warm summers and mild winters. This climate encourages outdoor activities and a love for al fresco dining. The city's food scene is a blend of international cuisines, with an emphasis on fresh, local produce. The bustling Eat Street Northshore is a food lover's paradise, offering a diverse range of culinary delights.

For sports enthusiasts, Brisbane has a strong sporting culture. The Gabba, a historic cricket ground, hosts international cricket matches and Australian rules football games. Suncorp Stadium, located in the inner city suburb of

Milton, is the venue for rugby league, rugby union, and soccer matches.

Beyond the city, the greater Brisbane region offers natural wonders to explore. The nearby Moreton Bay is a playground for water activities, from sailing and fishing to dolphin watching. The picturesque Sunshine Coast and Gold Coast are within easy reach, making Brisbane a gateway to some of Australia's most famous beaches.

In conclusion, Brisbane, the Sunshine State's Capital, is a city that embodies the warmth and optimism of Queensland. Its blend of natural beauty, cultural richness, and modernity creates a unique urban experience. Brisbane's welcoming spirit, combined with its commitment to arts, culture, and the outdoors, makes it a city that continues to shine as a vibrant and dynamic destination.

Perth: Gateway to the West

Perth, often referred to as the "Gateway to the West," is a city that occupies a unique place in Australia's geographical landscape. As the capital of Western Australia, Perth is not only the most isolated major city on the planet but also a thriving metropolis that boasts a lifestyle and culture all its own.

Located on the southwestern coast of Australia, Perth enjoys a Mediterranean climate, with warm, dry summers and mild, wet winters. Its climate is characterized by an abundance of sunshine, which has earned it the nickname "The City of Light." The city's residents savor the outdoors, and it's not uncommon to find them enjoying the many parks, beaches, and outdoor activities that Perth has to offer.

One of Perth's most defining features is its pristine coastline. Stretching for miles along the Indian Ocean, the city's beaches are among the best in the world. Cottesloe Beach, with its golden sands and clear waters, is a favorite spot for swimmers and sunbathers. Scarborough Beach is known for its surf and vibrant beachside atmosphere. Perth's beaches offer the perfect setting for leisurely picnics, water sports, and stunning sunsets.

Kings Park and Botanic Garden, located just west of the city center, is one of the largest inner-city parks in the world. It offers sweeping views of the Swan River and the city skyline. The park is home to a remarkable array of native flora and provides a tranquil escape from the urban hustle and bustle.

The Swan River itself is an integral part of Perth's identity. It meanders through the city, offering opportunities for boating, fishing, and riverside picnics. The river's banks are lined with parks and walking trails, making it a popular destination for both residents and tourists.

Perth's central business district (CBD) is a hub of commerce and culture. The city's skyline is dominated by modern skyscrapers, reflecting its status as a major economic center in Australia. The Perth Cultural Centre, located in the CBD, is home to institutions like the Art Gallery of Western Australia and the Western Australian Museum.

The city's culinary scene has evolved in recent years, with an emphasis on fresh, locally sourced ingredients. The Swan Valley, located just outside Perth, is Western Australia's oldest wine region, known for its vineyards and cellar doors. Perth's dining options are diverse, with a focus on seafood and international cuisines, reflecting the city's multicultural population.

Fremantle, often called "Freo" by locals, is a vibrant port city located just southwest of Perth. It has a rich maritime history and a charming historic district filled with shops, cafes, and markets. Fremantle is also known for its lively arts and music scene, making it a cultural destination in its own right.

Perth's isolation has fostered a unique sense of identity among its residents. The city has a relaxed pace of life, and many people are drawn to its laid-back atmosphere. Despite its geographical remoteness, Perth is well-connected to the rest of Australia through air travel and offers a gateway to exploring the vast landscapes of Western Australia, from the rugged beauty of the Kimberley to the pristine beaches of the Margaret River region.

In conclusion, Perth, the "Gateway to the West," is a city that embraces its isolation and celebrates the natural beauty of Western Australia. With its stunning beaches, vibrant arts scene, and outdoor lifestyle, Perth offers a unique and captivating experience for residents and visitors alike. It's a city that embodies the spirit of adventure and discovery, where the sun-drenched landscapes of the West are just waiting to be explored.

Adelaide: The City of Churches

Adelaide, often affectionately referred to as the "City of Churches," is a city of elegance, culture, and rich history. Nestled on the southern coast of Australia, it is the capital of South Australia and offers a unique blend of old-world charm and modern sophistication.

One of the city's most distinctive features is its collection of historic churches and cathedrals, which gave rise to its nickname. Adelaide's founders, British settlers in the early 19th century, had a vision of creating a city that celebrated religious freedom and tolerance. As a result, numerous churches were built, representing various denominations and architectural styles.

St. Peter's Cathedral, an Anglican masterpiece, is a stunning example of Gothic Revival architecture. Its spire soars into the sky and is a prominent feature of the city's skyline. The Church of St. Francis Xavier, a Catholic church, showcases exquisite stone masonry and stained glass windows, adding to the city's ecclesiastical charm.

Adelaide's layout is unique, with wide, tree-lined streets and an abundance of green spaces. This design was influenced by Colonel William Light, the city's planner, who envisioned a city with a focus on greenery and open spaces. The Adelaide Park Lands, a vast ring of parkland encircling the city center, provide a haven for outdoor activities, picnics, and leisurely strolls.

North Terrace, a grand boulevard, is home to some of Adelaide's most significant cultural institutions. The South

Australian Museum, the Art Gallery of South Australia, and the State Library of South Australia are all situated along this avenue. These institutions house extensive collections of art, cultural artifacts, and historical documents, providing a window into South Australia's heritage.

Adelaide's thriving arts scene extends beyond museums and galleries. The Adelaide Festival Centre is a premier venue for performing arts, hosting a diverse range of theater productions, musical performances, and dance shows. The Adelaide Fringe Festival, one of the world's largest arts festivals, takes over the city with an eclectic program of events and performances each year.

Adelaide is renowned for its food and wine culture. The Barossa Valley and McLaren Vale, located a short drive from the city, are internationally acclaimed wine regions known for their Shiraz and other varietals. Adelaide Central Market, a bustling food hub, offers an array of fresh produce, gourmet delights, and international cuisines. The city's dining scene is diverse, with a focus on farm-to-table and locally sourced ingredients.

Glenelg Beach, with its white sands and vibrant seaside atmosphere, is a popular destination for both locals and tourists. It's easily accessible from the city center via tram and provides a perfect setting for swimming, sunbathing, and water sports.

Adelaide's festivals are a testament to its cultural vibrancy. The Adelaide Festival of Arts, the WOMADelaide world music festival, and the Adelaide Film Festival are just a few of the annual events that celebrate the city's creative spirit.

Adelaide's climate is characterized by mild winters and warm, dry summers, making it an ideal destination year-round. The Mediterranean-like climate also contributes to the city's reputation for producing some of the country's finest produce and wines.

In conclusion, Adelaide, the "City of Churches," is a city of grace, culture, and historical significance. Its commitment to preserving its heritage while embracing modernity creates a unique urban experience. With its historic churches, cultural institutions, and vibrant arts scene, Adelaide continues to be a city that celebrates its rich past while looking forward to a bright future.

Hobart: Tasmania's Capital

Hobart, the capital city of Tasmania, is a place of natural beauty, maritime heritage, and a relaxed way of life. Situated on the southeastern coast of the island, Hobart is the second oldest capital city in Australia, and it exudes a distinct charm that reflects both its colonial history and its modern identity.

Nestled between the towering kunanyi/Mount Wellington and the sparkling waters of the Derwent River, Hobart's natural surroundings are awe-inspiring. The city's residents and visitors alike enjoy the proximity to outdoor adventures. Mount Wellington, with its panoramic views of the city and the surrounding wilderness, is a popular destination for hikers and nature enthusiasts.

Hobart's waterfront, known as Sullivans Cove, is a focal point of the city's identity. Here, historic sandstone warehouses have been transformed into cafes, restaurants, and galleries, creating a vibrant precinct known as Salamanca Place. The Salamanca Markets, held every Saturday, attract locals and tourists alike, offering a delightful array of arts, crafts, fresh produce, and gourmet foods.

The maritime heritage of Hobart is celebrated at the Tasmanian Museum and Art Gallery, located in the heart of the city. The museum showcases Tasmania's rich history, from its Aboriginal heritage to its colonial past, and features an impressive collection of art and artifacts. Hobart is also the gateway to exploring Tasmania's unique wilderness areas. The UNESCO World Heritage-listed Port Arthur Historic Site, a former penal colony, provides a window into Australia's convict history. Bruny Island, just a short ferry ride from Hobart, offers pristine beaches, rugged coastlines, and abundant wildlife, including the famous white wallabies. The city's food scene has flourished in recent years, with a focus on locally sourced produce. Hobart is known for its seafood, with fresh catches from the surrounding waters readily available. The Farm Gate Market, held every Sunday, is a showcase of Tasmania's finest artisanal produce, including cheeses, fruits, and gourmet goods.

Hobart's cultural life thrives with the annual MONA FOMA (Museum of Old and New Art - Festival of Music and Art) and the Tasmanian Symphony Orchestra, both contributing to the city's artistic vitality. The Museum of Old and New Art (MONA), located just a short ferry ride from the city center, is an avant-garde institution that houses a provocative collection of contemporary art.

The city's architecture reflects its historical past, with well-preserved Georgian and Victorian buildings lining the streets of Battery Point and other historic neighborhoods. The Royal Tasmanian Botanical Gardens, established in 1818, offer a serene oasis with a diverse collection of plants, including an extensive subantarctic plant house.

Hobart's climate is temperate, with mild summers and cool winters, making it an ideal destination year-round. The city's festivals and events, including the Taste of Tasmania food and wine festival and the Australian Wooden Boat Festival, add to its cultural vibrancy.

In conclusion, Hobart, Tasmania's capital, is a city that celebrates its natural beauty, history, and vibrant culture. It offers a unique blend of wilderness exploration, maritime heritage, and culinary delights. With its stunning surroundings and friendly atmosphere, Hobart invites visitors to embrace its laid-back charm and immerse themselves in the rich tapestry of Tasmania's capital city.

Canberra: Australia's Political Heart

Canberra, the purpose-built capital city of Australia, stands as a testament to the nation's democratic ideals and political unity. Nestled within the Australian Capital Territory (ACT), Canberra is a city unlike any other in the country, designed from the ground up to serve as the political and administrative center of Australia.

The city's genesis as the capital can be traced back to the Federation of Australia in 1901 when the six Australian colonies came together to form a single nation. A significant debate arose regarding the location of the nation's capital, ultimately leading to the compromise of creating a new capital rather than selecting one of the existing major cities, such as Sydney or Melbourne.

Canberra's location was chosen for several reasons. It was situated between the two largest cities, Sydney and Melbourne, to alleviate the rivalry between them. Additionally, it was positioned inland to reduce the vulnerability to naval attacks. American architect Walter Burley Griffin and his wife, Marion Mahony Griffin, won the international design competition to plan the city's layout, which was inspired by the principles of the Garden City movement and featured geometric patterns and natural landscapes. Construction of Canberra began in 1913, and the city officially became the capital in 1912, replacing Melbourne. One of the most iconic features of the city is Capitol Hill, which houses Australia's Parliament House. This striking building was designed by Romaldo Giurgola and opened in 1988. Its flagpole, standing at 81 meters (266 feet), is one of the world's largest stainless steel structures. Old Parliament House, now known as the Museum of Australian

Democracy, is another important historical site in Canberra. It served as the home of the Australian Parliament from 1927 until the opening of the new Parliament House. The National Library of Australia, the National Gallery of Australia, and the High Court of Australia are among the other significant institutions located in the parliamentary triangle of the city.

Beyond its political role, Canberra is a city with a strong emphasis on education and research. The Australian National University (ANU), founded in 1946, is ranked among the world's top universities and plays a pivotal role in shaping the nation's intellectual discourse. Canberra's design incorporates a network of open spaces, including Lake Burley Griffin, which serves both recreational and aesthetic purposes. The lake offers opportunities for sailing, kayaking, and picnicking, with walking and cycling paths along its shores.

The city's population includes a diverse mix of public servants, diplomats, academics, and residents from around the world. It is known for its clean and orderly streets, well-maintained parks, and a high standard of living. Canberra's climate is characterized by four distinct seasons, with warm summers and cold winters. The city's cultural calendar is marked by events such as Floriade, a vibrant flower festival held annually, and the Enlighten Festival, which illuminates the city's landmarks with colorful projections.

In conclusion, Canberra, Australia's Political Heart, is a city purposefully designed to house the nation's political institutions and embody its democratic values. It stands as a symbol of unity and governance, while also offering a high quality of life and a vibrant cultural scene. Canberra's unique status as the capital city underscores its significance in Australia's history and its ongoing role in shaping the nation's future.

Darwin: The Gateway to the Top End

Darwin, the capital of Australia's Northern Territory, is a city that stands as the gateway to the untamed wilderness of the Top End. Situated on the northern coast of the Australian continent, Darwin is a place where rugged landscapes meet vibrant multiculturalism, and where history and nature coexist in a unique balance.

The city's history is marked by its resilience and the impact of World War II. In 1942, Darwin endured devastating bombings by Japanese forces, leading to the reconstruction and expansion of the city in the post-war years. Today, remnants of this history can be explored at sites like the Darwin Military Museum and the iconic Stokes Hill Wharf.

Darwin's modern identity is shaped by its multicultural population, with a significant Indigenous presence and residents hailing from around the world. The city's markets, such as Mindil Beach Sunset Market and Parap Village Markets, offer a tantalizing array of international cuisines, reflecting this cultural diversity. Street food vendors and fresh seafood stalls are local favorites.

The tropical climate of Darwin is a defining feature, with a distinct wet and dry season. The wet season brings heavy rainfall and thunderstorms, while the dry season offers pleasant weather for outdoor activities. The city's proximity to the equator means that temperatures remain warm throughout the year, making it an ideal destination for those seeking a tropical escape.

Darwin's natural surroundings are a source of wonder and adventure. Kakadu National Park, a UNESCO World Heritage site, lies to the east and is known for its ancient Aboriginal rock art, wetlands teeming with wildlife, and stunning waterfalls. Litchfield National Park, to the southwest, is famous for its unique termite mounds and refreshing swimming holes.

One of Darwin's most iconic natural landmarks is the Tiwi Islands, located a short ferry ride from the city. These islands are home to the Tiwi people, known for their rich cultural traditions and vibrant art. Visitors can experience the Tiwi way of life through art workshops and cultural tours.

The waterfront precinct of Darwin boasts a bustling atmosphere, with restaurants, bars, and recreational areas. The Darwin Waterfront Wave Lagoon provides a safe and enjoyable place to swim, while the nearby Stokes Hill Wharf offers dining with panoramic views of the harbor.

The Darwin Festival, held annually, celebrates the city's arts and culture with a program of music, theater, and visual arts. The Darwin Waterfront Harmony Soiree and the Territory Day fireworks display are other popular events that showcase the city's lively spirit.

Darwin's proximity to Asia makes it a key hub for international trade and relations. The city's deep-water port is essential for the export of minerals, cattle, and other goods, contributing significantly to the region's economy.

In conclusion, Darwin, the Gateway to the Top End, is a city of contrasts, where a rich history meets a diverse and dynamic present. Its tropical climate, multicultural population, and stunning natural surroundings make it a unique destination for those seeking adventure, culture, and a taste of the Australian outback. Darwin embodies the spirit of the Top End, inviting travelers to explore the untamed beauty of northern Australia.

The Aboriginal Culture and Art

The Aboriginal culture of Australia is one of the oldest and most richly diverse in the world, with a history spanning tens of thousands of years. This ancient culture is deeply intertwined with the land, representing a profound connection between the Indigenous peoples of Australia and their environment.

Central to Aboriginal culture is the Dreamtime, also known as the Dreaming or the Songlines. It is a spiritual concept that encompasses the creation of the world and all living things within it. According to Dreamtime beliefs, ancestral beings known as "Dreamtime ancestors" traveled across the land, shaping the landscape, creating animals, plants, and humans, and leaving behind a spiritual essence. The Dreamtime is not just a creation story but a way of understanding the world, explaining natural phenomena, and passing down cultural knowledge through oral traditions.

Art plays a vital role in Aboriginal culture, serving as a medium for storytelling, connecting with the Dreamtime, and expressing the deep connection to the land. Aboriginal art is incredibly diverse, with distinct styles and techniques developed by different Indigenous groups across Australia. Some of the most renowned forms of Aboriginal art include dot painting, bark painting, and rock art.

Dot painting, characterized by intricate patterns of dots and symbols, is often used to depict Dreamtime stories and the landscapes associated with them. Each dot represents a specific element of the story, and the patterns may be layered to create depth and complexity. This form of art has gained international recognition and is highly sought after by collectors.

Bark painting is a traditional art form of Aboriginal communities in the Northern Territory, where designs are painted onto the inner bark of trees. These paintings often depict Dreamtime stories, animals, and plants. The choice of natural materials connects the art to the land and emphasizes the relationship between culture and environment.

Rock art is another significant aspect of Aboriginal art and cultural expression. These ancient paintings and engravings can be found across Australia, with some dating back tens of thousands of years. They often depict Dreamtime stories, hunting scenes, and spiritual symbols. Some of the most famous rock art sites include those in Kakadu National Park and the Kimberley region.

Aboriginal art isn't confined to paintings alone; it extends to various forms of creative expression, including dance, music, and storytelling. Traditional dance performances, often accompanied by the didgeridoo, convey cultural narratives and are an integral part of ceremonies and gatherings.

The didgeridoo, a wind instrument made from hollowed-out tree trunks, is synonymous with Indigenous music. Its deep, resonant sound has a spiritual significance and is used in storytelling and ceremonies.

Aboriginal storytelling is conveyed through oral traditions, where elders pass down knowledge, Dreamtime stories, and cultural practices to younger generations. These stories are a living history, connecting people to their ancestors and the land.

The significance of Aboriginal culture and art goes beyond aesthetics. It's a living testament to the resilience, wisdom, and enduring traditions of Australia's Indigenous peoples. Today, efforts are being made to preserve and celebrate this cultural heritage, ensuring that it continues to thrive for generations to come.

In conclusion, the Aboriginal culture and art of Australia are a testament to the deep spiritual connection between Indigenous peoples and the land. From the Dreamtime stories that explain the world's creation to the intricate art forms that convey these narratives, Aboriginal culture is a rich tapestry that reflects the history, spirituality, and enduring legacy of Australia's First Nations.

Modern Australian Art and Music

Modern Australian art and music are vibrant and dynamic expressions of the country's cultural diversity, history, and contemporary identity. Australia's creative scene has evolved over the years, reflecting both Indigenous and immigrant influences, and contributing to the global cultural landscape.

In the realm of visual arts, modern Australian art encompasses a wide range of styles, themes, and mediums. Indigenous art, with its roots in ancient traditions, has gained international recognition. Aboriginal artists, such as Emily Kame Kngwarreye and Albert Namatjira, have left an indelible mark on the art world, infusing their works with a deep connection to the land, Dreamtime stories, and cultural heritage.

Contemporary Indigenous artists continue to push boundaries, blending traditional techniques with innovative approaches. The use of vibrant colors, intricate dot paintings, and the depiction of Dreamtime narratives are hallmarks of contemporary Indigenous art. Artists like Sally Gabori and Lena Nyadbi have earned acclaim for their innovative interpretations of Indigenous art forms.

Beyond Indigenous art, modern Australian artists explore diverse themes, from the Australian landscape to social and political issues. The Australian landscape has been a recurring source of inspiration, captured in works by artists like Sidney Nolan, Arthur Boyd, and Fred Williams. These artists have reimagined the Australian terrain, showcasing its unique beauty and stark contrasts.

In the world of music, Australia has made significant contributions across various genres. Australian rock bands, such as AC/DC, INXS, and Men at Work, achieved international fame and left an indelible mark on the global music scene. AC/DC, in particular, is regarded as one of the greatest rock bands of all time.

The Australian alternative and indie music scene has also produced influential artists like Tame Impala, Nick Cave and the Bad Seeds, and Sia. Tame Impala, with its psychedelic soundscapes, has garnered critical acclaim and a dedicated fan base worldwide. Nick Cave's poetic lyrics and haunting melodies have earned him a devoted following, while Sia's powerful vocals and songwriting have made her an international pop sensation.

Australia's classical music tradition is exemplified by the Sydney Symphony Orchestra and the Melbourne Symphony Orchestra, both renowned for their performances of classical and contemporary compositions. The country's opera companies, such as Opera Australia, have produced world-class productions and nurtured local talent.

Electronic dance music (EDM) has also found a home in Australia, with festivals like Stereosonic and artists like Flume and Alison Wonderland gaining prominence in the global EDM scene. These artists have pushed the boundaries of electronic music, fusing it with diverse influences and creating a unique Australian sound.

Australia's multiculturalism is reflected in its music scene, with artists from diverse backgrounds contributing to its richness. Musicians like John Butler, Xavier Rudd, and Gurrumul Yunupingu draw on various musical traditions to create a fusion of styles that resonates with audiences both in Australia and abroad.

In recent years, the Australian music industry has faced challenges, particularly due to the impact of digital streaming and the COVID-19 pandemic. However, the resilience and creativity of Australian artists continue to shine through as they adapt to new ways of reaching their audiences.

In conclusion, modern Australian art and music are dynamic expressions of the country's cultural tapestry. From the ancient traditions of Indigenous art to the global influence of Australian rock bands, the creative landscape is a reflection of the nation's diversity, innovation, and enduring passion for artistic expression. Whether on canvas or through musical notes, Australia's artists continue to captivate and inspire the world.

Sporting Culture: Cricket, Rugby, and More

Australia's sporting culture runs deep, ingrained in the national psyche and celebrated on the world stage. From the green cricket fields to the rugged rugby pitches, and a myriad of other sports, Australians have a passion for both playing and watching their favorite games.

Cricket stands out as one of Australia's most cherished sports. The history of Australian cricket is intertwined with its identity. The Ashes rivalry against England is legendary, dating back to 1882 when Australia defeated England at The Oval, leading to the symbolic "death" of English cricket and the birth of the Ashes urn. Australian cricket greats like Sir Don Bradman and Shane Warne have achieved iconic status, with records and performances that are celebrated to this day. The Baggy Green, the Australian cricket team's cap, is a symbol of pride and excellence.

On the rugby front, Australia is a powerhouse in two distinct codes: rugby union and rugby league. Rugby union, epitomized by the Wallabies, has a rich tradition, with two Rugby World Cup victories to their name. The Bledisloe Cup clashes against New Zealand's All Blacks are eagerly anticipated battles. In contrast, rugby league boasts the National Rugby League (NRL), featuring teams like the Sydney Roosters, South Sydney Rabbitohs, and Queensland's State of Origin rivalry. The physicality and speed of rugby league attract a passionate following.

Australian Rules Football (AFL) is another sport that captivates the nation. The Australian Football League showcases teams like the Essendon Bombers, Collingwood Magpies, and Richmond Tigers. The AFL Grand Final is a major sporting event, drawing huge crowds to the Melbourne Cricket Ground (MCG) and watched by millions on television.

Soccer, or football as it's known internationally, has seen significant growth in Australia. The A-League features clubs like Sydney FC, Melbourne Victory, and Western Sydney Wanderers. The Matildas, Australia's women's national soccer team, has achieved remarkable success on the global stage, inspiring future generations.

Tennis is a sport where Australia has a storied history, with legends like Rod Laver and Margaret Court. The Australian Open, one of tennis' Grand Slam events, draws the world's top players to Melbourne Park each year.

In motorsports, the Australian Grand Prix is a fixture on the Formula 1 calendar. Bathurst 1000, a grueling endurance race, is a highlight for motorsport enthusiasts.

Sailing is part of Australia's DNA, with the Sydney to Hobart Yacht Race being a prestigious event in the sailing world. The America's Cup victory in 1983, breaking the United States' 132-year reign, remains a historic achievement.

In the realm of horse racing, the Melbourne Cup is known as "the race that stops a nation." Flemington Racecourse hosts this iconic event, attracting thoroughbreds and punters from around the world.

The culture of sportsmanship and fair play is deeply ingrained in Australian sports. Sporting heroes are celebrated not only for their skill but for their integrity and humility. The Aussie "fair go" spirit extends to both winners and losers, fostering a sense of camaraderie among fans.

Beyond the professional leagues, Australians of all ages and backgrounds actively participate in sports. Local cricket clubs, rugby teams, and community sports groups are hubs of social interaction and fitness.

In conclusion, Australia's sporting culture is a reflection of its passion for competition, physical prowess, and a commitment to excellence. Whether it's the hushed tension of a Test match at the Sydney Cricket Ground or the frenetic energy of an AFL Grand Final at the MCG, sports are an integral part of the Australian way of life, bringing people together and creating moments of triumph and camaraderie that resonate across the nation.

Indigenous Dreamtime Stories

Indigenous Dreamtime stories are the ancient narratives that underpin the spiritual and cultural beliefs of Australia's Aboriginal peoples. These stories, often referred to as Dreaming or Songlines, are not just tales of creation; they are the living, breathing foundation of Indigenous culture, connecting the past, present, and future.

At the heart of Dreamtime stories is the belief that the world was created by ancestral beings during a timeless period known as the Dreamtime. These ancestral beings, often depicted as animals, humans, or spirits, traveled across the land, shaping the landscape, creating animals, plants, and humans, and leaving behind a spiritual essence.

The Dreamtime narratives vary across different Indigenous groups, reflecting the diversity of cultures and languages across Australia. These stories are passed down orally from generation to generation, ensuring the preservation of cultural knowledge and spiritual connection to the land.

One of the most iconic Dreamtime stories is that of the Rainbow Serpent, a powerful and creative ancestral being that played a significant role in shaping the land and waterways. The Rainbow Serpent is often associated with waterholes, rivers, and the creation of water sources in the arid Australian landscape.

Another well-known Dreamtime narrative is the story of Tiddalik the Frog, who drank all the water in the world, leading to a crisis for the other animals. Through teamwork and clever strategies, the animals were able to make

Tiddalik laugh, causing him to release the water and restore balance to the world.

Dreamtime stories also explain natural phenomena and provide guidance on living harmoniously with the land. They offer insights into hunting, gathering, and traditional practices, emphasizing the importance of respecting the land and its resources.

These stories are not static; they continue to evolve and adapt to contemporary contexts. Indigenous artists use Dreamtime narratives as inspiration for their artwork, creating paintings that depict ancestral beings and the land. These artworks not only serve as a visual representation of the stories but also contribute to the preservation of cultural heritage.

The concept of Songlines is integral to Dreamtime stories. Songlines are intricate maps that connect places, stories, and songs, allowing Indigenous people to navigate vast landscapes, pass on cultural knowledge, and mark significant sites. These Songlines are a vital part of Indigenous identity and spirituality.

The importance of Dreamtime stories extends beyond cultural significance; they also hold legal and environmental importance. In some cases, Dreamtime narratives have been used in land rights claims, reinforcing the Indigenous connection to the land. Additionally, these stories often contain ecological knowledge that contributes to sustainable land management practices.

While Dreamtime stories are deeply rooted in tradition, they remain relevant in contemporary Indigenous life. They provide a sense of identity, belonging, and purpose, fostering resilience and pride among Indigenous communities. The stories are a reminder that the connection between people, land, and culture is a living and enduring one.

In conclusion, Indigenous Dreamtime stories are the ancient narratives that shape the spiritual and cultural identity of Australia's Aboriginal peoples. They are a testament to the enduring connection between Indigenous communities and the land, offering insights into creation, spirituality, and the ongoing journey of cultural preservation and adaptation. These stories are a treasure trove of wisdom, creativity, and spirituality that continue to resonate across the Australian landscape.

Australian Festivals and Celebrations

Australia is a land of diverse cultures and landscapes, and this diversity is celebrated through a wide array of festivals and celebrations that showcase the nation's rich tapestry of traditions, arts, and heritage. From ancient Indigenous ceremonies to contemporary multicultural festivals, Australia offers a calendar full of vibrant and meaningful events.

One of the most iconic celebrations in Australia is Australia Day, observed on January 26th. It marks the anniversary of the arrival of the First Fleet in 1788, an event seen by some as the founding of modern Australia. While it's a day of national pride and fireworks, it also sparks discussions about the treatment of Indigenous peoples and their connection to the land.

Indigenous festivals and ceremonies are deeply rooted in the land's spiritual and cultural traditions. The Garma Festival in Arnhem Land and the Laura Dance Festival in Queensland are examples of gatherings that celebrate Indigenous culture through song, dance, art, and storytelling. These events provide a platform for the sharing of Dreamtime stories, preserving cultural knowledge, and fostering understanding.

The Sydney Gay and Lesbian Mardi Gras is a globally renowned celebration of LGBTQIA+ pride and diversity. It features a colorful parade, parties, and performances, attracting visitors from around the world. This festival also has a history of activism and advocacy for LGBTQIA+ rights.

Vivid Sydney is an annual light, music, and ideas festival that transforms the city's landmarks into stunning light installations. It's a celebration of creativity and innovation, merging art, technology, and music to create a mesmerizing experience for locals and tourists alike.

Chinese New Year is a significant cultural festival celebrated with gusto in Australia's Chinese communities. Sydney's Chinatown becomes a hub of vibrant performances, dragon and lion dances, and delectable Chinese cuisine. It's a time to honor traditions, family, and good fortune.

Easter is marked by various events, including the Royal Easter Show in Sydney, which showcases agriculture, entertainment, and the Australian way of life. The Great Australian Barbie, a barbecue feast, is a quintessential way to celebrate Easter.

Anzac Day, observed on April 25th, commemorates the sacrifices of Australian and New Zealand soldiers in wars and conflicts. Dawn services, parades, and the playing of the Last Post are poignant moments of remembrance.

The Melbourne Cup, known as "the race that stops a nation," is Australia's most prestigious horse race. It's celebrated with horse races, glamorous fashion, and a public holiday in Victoria.

Multicultural festivals are a testament to Australia's diverse population. The Diwali Festival of Lights, Greek Glendi, and Italian Festa are just a few examples of cultural festivals that showcase the traditions, music, dance, and culinary delights of various communities.

The Woodford Folk Festival is a massive celebration of music, arts, and ideas held annually in Queensland. It brings together artists, musicians, and thinkers for a week of creativity and exploration.

Festivals in regional areas also have their unique charm, such as the Tamworth Country Music Festival, celebrating Australia's country music heritage, and the Taste of Tasmania in Hobart, highlighting the island state's culinary delights.

Australia's festivals and celebrations reflect the nation's values of inclusivity, creativity, and a love for the outdoors. They provide opportunities to learn about different cultures, appreciate Indigenous traditions, and come together as a community. These events are a vibrant expression of what it means to be Australian in a diverse and interconnected world.

Australian Etiquette and Customs

Understanding Australian etiquette and customs is key to making a positive impression when visiting this diverse and welcoming nation. Australians are known for their laid-back and friendly demeanor, but like any culture, there are certain norms and practices to be aware of.

1. Greetings: Australians tend to be informal when it comes to greetings. A simple "G'day" or "Hello" is common. Handshakes are the typical form of greeting in business and social settings. In more relaxed situations, you may encounter the friendly Aussie hug or cheek kiss.
2. Punctuality: Being on time is appreciated in Australia, especially in professional and formal contexts. It's considered polite to arrive punctually for meetings, appointments, and social gatherings.
3. Informality: Australians generally prefer a casual and informal approach to interactions. First names are commonly used, even in professional settings. However, it's still advisable to wait for an invitation to use someone's first name, especially in business.
4. Personal Space: Australians value personal space. It's important to respect people's physical boundaries and avoid standing too close during conversations, unless you have a close relationship with them.
5. Tipping: Tipping is not as common in Australia as it is in some other countries. In restaurants, it's customary to leave a tip if you receive exceptional service, but it's not obligatory. Wages for service

staff are generally higher in Australia than in places where tipping is expected.

6. Table Manners: When dining in someone's home or at a restaurant, good table manners are appreciated. Wait for everyone to be served before eating, and keep your elbows off the table. If you're invited to someone's home, it's customary to bring a bottle of wine or a small gift for the host.

7. Gift Giving: Giving and receiving gifts is common for birthdays, holidays, and special occasions. It's considered thoughtful to bring a gift when invited to someone's home. Australians appreciate practical gifts and those that reflect their interests.

8. Small Talk: Australians are known for their skill in engaging in small talk. Weather, sports, and current events are safe and popular topics. Australians enjoy discussing their country's natural beauty and outdoor activities.

9. Sense of Humor: Australians have a renowned sense of humor, often characterized by self-deprecation and light-hearted banter. Be prepared for jokes and sarcasm, but always remember to keep it respectful and avoid sensitive topics.

10. Beach Culture: Australia's stunning beaches are an integral part of the culture. Beachgoers are expected to follow safety rules, like swimming between the flags at patrolled beaches. Sun protection is essential due to the harsh Australian sun.

11. Multiculturalism: Australia is a multicultural society, and respecting cultural diversity is crucial. Australians are generally open and accepting of different cultures, so be open-minded and curious about others' backgrounds.

12. Indigenous Respect: When visiting Indigenous communities or culturally significant sites, it's

important to show respect and follow any cultural protocols or restrictions. Seek permission before taking photos in these areas.

13. Driving Etiquette: Australians drive on the left side of the road. Seatbelts are mandatory for all passengers, and mobile phone use while driving is prohibited. Follow speed limits and road rules diligently.

14. Alcohol Consumption: Australians enjoy socializing over a drink, but excessive drinking is frowned upon. Drink responsibly, especially in public spaces.

15. No Smoking Zones: Smoking is prohibited in many public places, including restaurants, bars, public transport, and some outdoor areas. Always check for designated smoking areas.

By familiarizing yourself with Australian etiquette and customs, you'll be better prepared to engage with locals, make friends, and enjoy your time in this vast and welcoming country. Australians value respect, politeness, and a friendly attitude, so embrace the culture and make the most of your Australian experience.

Australian Slang and Language

Australia is a land of linguistic quirks and unique slang that can leave visitors scratching their heads. While English is the official language, Australians have a way of putting their own spin on it, resulting in a distinctive and colorful vocabulary. Here's a dive into the world of Australian slang and language.

1. G'day: You'll often hear Australians greet each other with a hearty "G'day." It's short for "good day" and is a quintessential Aussie salutation.
2. Mate: Australians are known for their friendliness, and they frequently refer to friends and acquaintances as "mate." It's an all-purpose term of camaraderie.
3. Arvo: Short for "afternoon," "arvo" is used to talk about anything happening later in the day. "See you this arvo!"
4. Barbie: Instead of a barbecue, Australians love to call it a "barbie." Firing up the barbie for a weekend cookout is a common tradition.
5. Brekkie: Australians have a fondness for abbreviating words, and "brekkie" is no exception. It's a casual term for breakfast.
6. Thongs: No, not the undergarments, but rather flip-flops or sandals. Australians wear "thongs" on their feet, especially in the warm climate.
7. Servo: When you need to fill up your car with petrol (gasoline), head to the "servo," short for service station.
8. Maccas: If you're craving a fast-food burger from McDonald's, just ask for "Maccas."
9. Chockers: When something is really full or crowded, it's described as "chockers." The train during rush hour can be chockers.

10. Bottle-O: If you're looking for a bottle shop or liquor store, ask for directions to the "bottle-o."

11. Bogan: A "bogan" is a term for someone who is seen as unsophisticated or with poor taste. It's often used humorously.

12. Ripper: When something is fantastic or excellent, Australians might exclaim, "That's a ripper!"

13. Sheila: An old-fashioned slang term for a woman. While not as common today, you might still hear it occasionally.

14. Fair Dinkum: This phrase means something is genuine or authentic. "Are you fair dinkum?" is a way of asking if someone is telling the truth.

15. No Worries: Australians are laid-back and often respond with "no worries" to express that everything is okay or to reassure someone.

16. Cuppa: Australians love their tea or coffee, and a "cuppa" simply means a cup of either.

17. Sanger: Short for "sandwich," "sanger" is a quick way to refer to a sandwich, often enjoyed for lunch.

18. Brewno: Australians have a penchant for creating slang words, and "brewno" is an affectionate way to refer to a close friend.

19. Cactus: When something is broken or not working, it's "cactus." "My phone's cactus, mate."

20. Chuck a U-ey: To make a U-turn while driving, Australians might say they're going to "chuck a U-ey."

These are just a few examples of Australian slang and language, and there are many more regional variations and idioms to discover. Embracing the local lingo can be a fun way to immerse yourself in Australian culture and strike up conversations with the friendly locals. So, whether you're heading to the beach with your "thongs" or enjoying a "barbie" with your "mates," you're sure to pick up some Aussie slang along the way.

Australian English: A Unique Dialect

Australian English is a vibrant and distinct dialect that has evolved over centuries, shaped by the nation's history, geography, and multicultural influences. While it's fundamentally rooted in British English, Australian English has developed its own identity, complete with unique vocabulary, pronunciation, and idiomatic expressions.

One of the most recognizable features of Australian English is its pronunciation. The accent, often referred to as the "Aussie accent," is characterized by its relaxed and somewhat nasal quality. Vowels are pronounced differently compared to other English dialects. For instance, the "i" sound in words like "bike" and "time" is pronounced more like "oi," resulting in "boik" and "toim."

Another notable feature is the phenomenon known as "strine," which is a playful term for Australian slang and colloquialisms. Australians are known for abbreviating words and adding a touch of humor to their language. Phrases like "G'day, mate," "No worries," and "How ya goin'?" are part of everyday conversation.

Australian English also has a distinct lexicon that reflects the nation's unique culture and environment. For example, "bush" refers to the vast, sparsely populated areas of the Australian outback. "Outback" itself is an Australian term for remote and rural areas. "Billabong" denotes a small pond or waterhole, often associated with Indigenous culture. The influence of Indigenous languages on Australian English is also evident in the names of flora, fauna, and geographical features. Words like "kangaroo," "koala," and "boomerang" are borrowed from Indigenous languages. The rich history of immigration has left its mark on the language as well. British, Irish, Scottish, and Welsh immigrants have contributed to the vocabulary and pronunciation of Australian English. Additionally, the Gold Rush era in the 19th century brought an influx of Chinese immigrants who left their linguistic imprint.

In recent decades, Australia's multiculturalism has further enriched the language. Words and phrases from languages such as Greek, Italian, Arabic, and Vietnamese have made their way into Australian English, especially in urban areas with diverse communities.

Australian English also exhibits a strong connection to the nation's outdoor lifestyle. Words like "barbie" (barbecue), "esky" (cooler box), and "thongs" (flip-flops) reflect the love for outdoor activities and the beach culture.

The influence of sports, particularly cricket and Australian rules football, can't be overstated. Australians have coined specific terms and expressions related to these sports, such as "sixer" (a cricket term for a boundary hit), "Aussie rules" (referring to Australian rules football), and "footy" (a common term for football).

In summary, Australian English is a unique dialect that reflects the nation's history, geography, multiculturalism, and outdoor lifestyle. Its distinct pronunciation, rich slang, and borrowed words from Indigenous languages and immigrant communities make it a fascinating linguistic tapestry. While firmly rooted in British English, Australian English stands on its own as an essential part of the nation's identity and culture.

Aboriginal Languages and Preservation Efforts

The rich tapestry of Indigenous cultures in Australia encompasses a remarkable diversity of languages, each carrying centuries of knowledge, stories, and traditions. These languages, collectively known as Aboriginal languages, are an integral part of the continent's history and heritage. However, the survival of many of these languages has been threatened over the years, prompting concerted efforts to preserve and revitalize them.

Australia is believed to have been inhabited by Indigenous peoples for over 60,000 years, making it one of the oldest continuous cultures on Earth. During this extensive period, hundreds of distinct languages and dialects developed across the continent, reflecting the deep connection between Indigenous communities and their ancestral lands.

One of the defining features of Aboriginal languages is their incredible diversity. There are estimated to be around 250 distinct Indigenous languages spoken in Australia at the time of European contact. These languages vary significantly in structure, vocabulary, and phonetics, reflecting the vast geographical and cultural differences among Indigenous groups.

The arrival of European settlers in the late 18th century had a profound impact on these languages. The imposition of English, along with disease, displacement, and other factors, led to a rapid decline in the use of many Aboriginal languages. As a result, numerous languages faced the risk of extinction.

Efforts to preserve and revitalize Aboriginal languages began in earnest in the latter half of the 20th century. Indigenous communities, linguists, and government organizations recognized the urgent need to document and protect these linguistic treasures. Several key initiatives have played a pivotal role in this preservation journey:

1. **Language Documentation:** Linguists and researchers have worked closely with Indigenous communities to document and record their languages. This involves recording oral histories, stories, and songs, as well as developing written versions of languages that were previously unwritten.
2. **Language Revitalization:** Language revitalization programs have been established to reintroduce Aboriginal languages into daily life. These programs often focus on teaching languages to younger generations through immersion programs, schools, and community activities.
3. **Language Centers:** Language centers have been established in various Indigenous communities, serving as hubs for language preservation efforts. These centers provide resources, training, and support for language revival initiatives.
4. **Collaboration:** Collaboration between Indigenous communities, linguists, and government bodies has been crucial in ensuring the success of language preservation efforts. Local knowledge and expertise are central to these collaborations.
5. **Cultural Significance:** Aboriginal languages are not merely a means of communication but also

repositories of cultural knowledge, spirituality, and identity. Their preservation is essential for the continuation of Indigenous cultures and traditions.

Despite the challenges, there have been heartening successes in recent years. Some languages once on the brink of extinction have experienced revitalization, with younger generations taking an active interest in learning and speaking their ancestral languages. This progress is a testament to the resilience and determination of Indigenous communities.

While the journey to preserve and revitalize Aboriginal languages is ongoing, it represents a crucial step toward acknowledging and respecting the cultural heritage of Australia's First Nations. These languages are not just words but living connections to the past, present, and future of Indigenous peoples, and their preservation is an essential part of reconciliation and cultural understanding in Australia.

Australian Education System

The Australian education system is known for its quality, diversity, and commitment to providing students with a well-rounded education. From early childhood education to higher education, it offers a range of options to cater to the needs and interests of students. Here, we'll take a comprehensive look at the Australian education system.

Early Childhood Education: The Australian education journey often begins with early childhood education and care. This stage is essential for the social, cognitive, and emotional development of children. It includes programs like kindergarten and childcare services, catering to children from infancy to about five years of age.

Primary Education: Primary education in Australia typically covers six years, from ages six to twelve. Students attend primary school, where they receive a foundational education in subjects such as English, mathematics, science, and social studies. Primary education emphasizes literacy and numeracy skills.

Secondary Education: Secondary education extends from ages twelve to eighteen and usually includes seven years of schooling. Students attend secondary schools, where they follow a diverse curriculum. In the later years, they have the option to specialize in subjects of their choice. The final two years of secondary education are particularly crucial, as students prepare for tertiary education or employment.

Tertiary Education: Australia is home to world-class universities, vocational education and training (VET) institutions, and technical and further education (TAFE) colleges. Tertiary education options are diverse, catering to a wide range of career aspirations. Australian universities are renowned for their academic excellence and research contributions.

Vocational Education and Training (VET): VET programs are practical and skill-focused, designed to prepare students for specific careers. These programs offer qualifications such as certificates, diplomas, and advanced diplomas. VET institutions work closely with industries to ensure graduates are job-ready.

Technical and Further Education (TAFE): TAFE colleges provide a broad spectrum of vocational courses. They offer training in areas like hospitality, automotive, healthcare, and more. TAFE qualifications are highly regarded by employers.

Higher Education: Australian universities consistently rank among the top in the world. They offer bachelor's, master's, and doctoral degrees across various fields. Higher education in Australia attracts students from around the globe due to its academic rigor and cultural diversity.

Quality Assurance: The Australian education system is known for its high standards and rigorous quality assurance processes. The Tertiary Education Quality and Standards Agency (TEQSA) monitors and ensures the quality of higher education institutions.

International Students: Australia is a popular destination for international students. Its universities and institutions welcome students from diverse backgrounds, creating a vibrant and multicultural learning environment.

Education Funding: Education in Australia is funded through a combination of government funding and private contributions. The government provides significant support for public education, ensuring accessibility and affordability.

Indigenous Education: Efforts are ongoing to improve education outcomes for Indigenous Australians. Initiatives aim to bridge the education gap and promote cultural awareness and respect.

Inclusivity: The Australian education system places a strong emphasis on inclusivity and support for students with diverse needs. Specialized programs and resources are available for students with disabilities and those facing socio-economic challenges.

In conclusion, the Australian education system is marked by its inclusivity, quality, and diversity. It offers a wide range of educational pathways to suit individual interests and career goals. Whether you're pursuing higher education, vocational training, or primary and secondary schooling, Australia provides a supportive and enriching learning environment for students of all ages.

Australian Healthcare and Social Services

Australia boasts a comprehensive healthcare system that is the envy of many nations. It's a system built on the principles of universality, accessibility, and quality care. In this chapter, we will delve into the intricacies of the Australian healthcare system and the social services that support the well-being of its citizens.

Universal Healthcare: At the core of Australia's healthcare system is Medicare, a government-funded initiative that provides universal access to healthcare services for all Australian citizens and permanent residents. Under Medicare, citizens are entitled to subsidized medical services, including doctor's visits, hospital stays, and certain diagnostic tests.

General Practitioners (GPs): General practitioners play a pivotal role in the healthcare system. Australians have the freedom to choose their GP, and consultations are typically bulk-billed through Medicare, meaning no out-of-pocket expenses for patients in most cases.

Hospitals: Australia boasts a network of public and private hospitals. Public hospitals provide healthcare services to all Australians at no or minimal cost, with charges often covered by Medicare. Private hospitals offer additional services for those with private health insurance, providing more choices for elective procedures and shorter waiting times.

Pharmaceutical Benefits Scheme (PBS): The PBS ensures affordable access to a wide range of prescription medications. Under this scheme, Australians pay a capped fee for prescription medicines, with the government covering the remaining cost.

Private Health Insurance: While Medicare provides essential healthcare coverage, many Australians opt for private health insurance to access additional benefits, including choice of doctor and shorter wait times for elective surgeries. Private health insurance is encouraged through government incentives.

Mental Health Services: Australia places a strong emphasis on mental health care. Services are available through both the public and private sectors, with a focus on early intervention, prevention, and community support.

Aged Care: Australia provides a comprehensive system of aged care services for its elderly population. This includes residential aged care facilities and in-home care options to support seniors in their preferred living arrangements.

Disability Services: The National Disability Insurance Scheme (NDIS) is a groundbreaking initiative that supports Australians with disabilities. It provides funding for personalized care plans and services, empowering individuals to lead fulfilling lives.

Social Services: Beyond healthcare, Australia offers an array of social services to support its citizens. These include unemployment benefits, family support payments, and programs to assist those facing financial hardship. The goal is to provide a safety net and promote social inclusion.

Indigenous Health: Efforts are ongoing to improve Indigenous health outcomes and address disparities. Initiatives focus on culturally sensitive healthcare services and community engagement.

Preventive Health: Australia places a strong emphasis on preventive health measures, including public health campaigns to encourage healthy lifestyles, vaccinations, and cancer screening programs.

Emergency Services: Australia's healthcare system is well-prepared for emergencies, including natural disasters and public health crises. Robust emergency response systems are in place to ensure the safety and well-being of citizens.

In summary, Australia's healthcare and social services are founded on principles of equity and access. The country's universal healthcare system, supported by Medicare, ensures that essential medical services are available to all citizens. Additionally, a range of social services provides support and assistance to individuals and families in various life circumstances. Australia's commitment to the well-being of its citizens is evident in the comprehensive and inclusive nature of its healthcare and social service systems.

Transport and Travel in Australia

Australia, a vast continent characterized by diverse landscapes, presents a unique set of challenges and opportunities when it comes to transportation and travel. Covering an area almost as large as the continental United States, Australia's transportation infrastructure has evolved to connect its major cities, remote outback regions, and everything in between.

Road Travel: Road travel is a popular choice for both domestic and international tourists exploring Australia. The country boasts a network of well-maintained highways and roads that connect major cities and regional centers. The most famous of these is the iconic Stuart Highway, stretching from Adelaide in the south to Darwin in the north, passing through the heart of the continent.

Rail Travel: Australia offers a unique rail travel experience. The Indian Pacific, The Ghan, and The Overland are renowned long-distance trains that traverse the country from coast to coast. These journeys provide passengers with breathtaking views of Australia's landscapes, from the arid Outback to lush coastal areas.

Domestic Flights: Due to the vast distances between cities, domestic flights are a common mode of transport for travelers. Australia has a well-developed domestic airline industry, with major carriers connecting cities and regional airports. Sydney, Melbourne, Brisbane, and Perth serve as major aviation hubs.

Regional and Remote Travel: Travelers seeking to explore the remote and wild beauty of Australia can access these areas via chartered flights, 4WD vehicles, or guided tours. The Australian Outback, Northern Territory, and Western Australia offer unique adventures for those with an appetite for exploration.

Public Transportation: Major cities like Sydney, Melbourne, Brisbane, and Perth have efficient public transportation systems, including buses, trams, trains, and ferries. These systems provide convenient options for getting around within urban areas.

Cycling and Walking: Australia's cities promote active transportation through cycling lanes and pedestrian-friendly pathways. Many cities, including Melbourne and Sydney, have embraced bike-sharing programs, making it easy for tourists to explore on two wheels.

Ferries and Water Travel: Australia's stunning coastline and waterways offer opportunities for travel by ferry. Iconic destinations like the Great Barrier Reef and Tasmania can be accessed via ferry services. Water taxis and cruises are also popular for exploring scenic coastal areas.

Car Rentals: Renting a car is a convenient way to explore Australia at your own pace. Rental companies operate in major cities and airports, providing a wide range of vehicles to suit different needs and budgets.

Travel Safety: Travelers in Australia can expect a high level of safety on the roads, in public transportation, and across the country in general. Australia has strict road safety regulations and standards in place.

Unique Landscapes: One of the most compelling aspects of travel in Australia is its ever-changing landscapes. From the lush rainforests of Queensland to the rugged terrain of the Australian Alps, the country offers a stunning array of natural beauty.

Indigenous Tourism: Australia's Indigenous cultures are an integral part of the country's identity. Travelers can engage in Indigenous tourism experiences that offer insights into the rich history, traditions, and art of Indigenous communities.

In conclusion, Australia's vastness and diversity make it a unique and captivating destination for travelers. Whether you're exploring its cosmopolitan cities, embarking on a cross-country train journey, or venturing into the remote Outback, Australia's transportation options cater to a wide range of interests and adventures. The country's commitment to safety, infrastructure development, and preserving its natural beauty ensures that travel in Australia is an experience like no other.

Environmental Conservation in Australia

Australia, with its diverse ecosystems, unique wildlife, and stunning landscapes, places a significant emphasis on environmental conservation. The nation recognizes the importance of preserving its natural heritage for current and future generations. This chapter explores the various aspects of environmental conservation in Australia, highlighting its commitment to safeguarding the environment.

Biodiversity Conservation: Australia is renowned for its exceptional biodiversity, with a wide range of native species found nowhere else on Earth. Conservation efforts aim to protect these unique flora and fauna, including iconic animals like kangaroos, koalas, and the Tasmanian devil. National parks, wildlife reserves, and protected areas play a crucial role in preserving natural habitats.

Great Barrier Reef: The Great Barrier Reef, one of the world's most significant marine ecosystems, is a UNESCO World Heritage site. Conservation initiatives focus on reducing pollution, regulating fishing, and addressing climate change impacts to protect this fragile coral reef system.

Land Conservation: Australia is committed to land conservation through initiatives such as the National Reserve System. This system aims to establish a comprehensive network of protected areas that encompass various ecosystems and landscapes, from rainforests to deserts.

Threatened Species: Australia acknowledges the challenges posed by habitat loss, invasive species, and climate change to its unique wildlife. Programs like the Threatened Species Strategy work toward the recovery of endangered species and their habitats.

Indigenous Land Management: Indigenous Australians have a deep connection to the land and have practiced sustainable land management for thousands of years. Collaborative efforts between Indigenous communities and conservation organizations promote traditional land management techniques and biodiversity conservation.

Climate Action: Australia is actively addressing climate change by participating in international agreements like the Paris Agreement. Initiatives focus on reducing greenhouse gas emissions, transitioning to renewable energy sources, and implementing climate adaptation strategies.

Waste Management: Waste reduction and recycling programs are prevalent across the country. Australia aims to minimize waste generation and promote responsible waste disposal to protect the environment.

Water Conservation: Managing water resources is critical in the arid regions of Australia. Water conservation efforts include efficient irrigation practices, water recycling, and measures to preserve freshwater ecosystems.

Environmental Education: Promoting environmental awareness and education is a key component of conservation efforts. Schools, community organizations, and government initiatives aim to instill a sense of responsibility for the environment in future generations.

Marine Conservation: Beyond the Great Barrier Reef, marine conservation efforts encompass the protection of marine species, prevention of overfishing, and conservation of coastal habitats.

Bushfire Management: Australia faces bushfire challenges, exacerbated by changing climate patterns. Strategies for bushfire management include controlled burns, early warning systems, and community preparedness.

International Collaboration: Australia collaborates with other nations on global environmental issues, such as migratory bird conservation and the protection of Antarctica's ecosystems.

In summary, Australia's commitment to environmental conservation is evident in its comprehensive approach to protecting its unique natural heritage. From preserving biodiversity and iconic ecosystems to addressing climate change and sustainable land management, Australia recognizes the importance of safeguarding the environment for the benefit of all. The nation's dedication to these efforts reflects its deep appreciation for the beauty and significance of its natural landscapes and wildlife.

Indigenous Rights and Reconciliation

Australia's journey toward recognizing and addressing the rights of its Indigenous peoples and fostering reconciliation is a complex and ongoing process deeply rooted in history, culture, and social justice. This chapter explores the multifaceted issues surrounding Indigenous rights and the nation's commitment to reconciliation.

Indigenous History: Indigenous peoples have inhabited Australia for over 65,000 years, maintaining rich cultures, languages, and traditions. Their connection to the land is fundamental to their identity.

Colonization and Dispossession: The arrival of European settlers in the late 18th century marked a turbulent period in Indigenous history. The dispossession of land, disease, violence, and forced removals had devastating impacts on Indigenous communities.

Stolen Generations: One of the most painful chapters in Australia's history is the forced removal of Indigenous children from their families, known as the Stolen Generations. This policy, aimed at assimilation, caused profound trauma and continues to have intergenerational effects.

1967 Referendum: In 1967, a historic referendum saw an overwhelming majority of Australians vote in favor of amending the constitution to include Indigenous people in the census and grant the federal government the power to legislate for Indigenous people.

Land Rights: Land rights movements, such as the Gurindji Strike and the Mabo case, paved the way for Indigenous land rights recognition. The Native Title Act of 1993 acknowledged Indigenous land rights and native title.

Reconciliation: The journey toward reconciliation acknowledges historical injustices and seeks to build respectful relationships between Indigenous and non-Indigenous Australians. The Council for Aboriginal Reconciliation, established in 1991, played a pivotal role in this process.

Apology to the Stolen Generations: In 2008, then-Prime Minister Kevin Rudd delivered a formal apology to the Stolen Generations on behalf of the Australian government, acknowledging the pain and suffering caused by these policies.

Closing the Gap: The Closing the Gap initiative aims to reduce disparities in health, education, and employment between Indigenous and non-Indigenous Australians. This ongoing effort involves collaboration between governments and Indigenous communities.

Recognition in the Constitution: There are ongoing discussions about recognizing Indigenous peoples in the Australian Constitution. This constitutional reform would acknowledge their unique place in the nation's history.

Cultural Revival: Indigenous cultures and languages are celebrated and preserved through various initiatives, including cultural festivals, language programs, and art exhibitions.

Self-Determination: Empowering Indigenous communities to make decisions about their own future is a core principle of reconciliation. Programs support self-governance and economic development.

Justice Reforms: Efforts are underway to address overrepresentation of Indigenous people in the criminal justice system and improve access to culturally sensitive legal services.

Truth-Telling: The importance of truth-telling and acknowledging the full extent of historical injustices is recognized as an essential step toward reconciliation.

Community-Led Solutions: Many successful reconciliation initiatives are driven by Indigenous communities themselves, emphasizing the importance of local knowledge and community-led solutions.

In conclusion, Australia's journey toward Indigenous rights recognition and reconciliation is marked by both progress and ongoing challenges. The nation's commitment to acknowledging historical injustices, empowering Indigenous communities, and fostering respectful relationships between all Australians reflects a shared aspiration for a more inclusive and equitable future. While the path may be long and complex, the pursuit of justice, healing, and reconciliation remains a fundamental aspect of Australia's national identity.

The Stolen Generations and Apology

One of the most somber chapters in Australian history revolves around the painful and heart-wrenching story of the Stolen Generations, a dark period that left an indelible mark on the nation's conscience. This chapter delves into the historical background, the harrowing experiences of Indigenous families, and the long-awaited apology that aimed to acknowledge the immense suffering caused by these policies.

The Stolen Generations refer to a period spanning over a century, from the late 1800s well into the 20th century, during which Australian governments, both state and federal, implemented policies and practices that led to the forced removal of Indigenous children from their families and communities. This policy was pursued under the premise of assimilation, with the belief that separating Indigenous children from their culture and heritage would lead to their integration into the broader Australian society.

The methods used to implement these policies were often traumatic and brutal. Children, some as young as babies, were forcibly taken from their families by government authorities, welfare agencies, or religious missions. These children were separated from their parents, grandparents, and siblings, often without any warning or explanation. The consequences of these forced removals were devastating. Families were torn apart, and the children suffered immeasurable trauma, both at the time of their removal and throughout their lives. They were subjected to cultural dislocation, loss of identity, and often suffered physical, emotional, and sexual abuse in institutions where they were placed. The Stolen Generations' impact extended across generations, with profound and lasting effects on Indigenous individuals, families, and communities. Many of those who were forcibly removed faced a lifetime of challenges, including struggles with identity, mental health, substance abuse, and disrupted family connections.

For decades, the stories of the Stolen Generations were silenced, and the pain was largely unrecognized by mainstream Australia. However, as the nation began to confront its history and acknowledge the wrongs of the past, calls for an official apology gained momentum.

On February 13, 2008, in a historic and emotionally charged moment, then-Prime Minister Kevin Rudd delivered a formal apology to the Stolen Generations on behalf of the Australian government. In a speech to the Australian Parliament, he expressed deep regret and sorrow for the pain and suffering inflicted on Indigenous families and communities through these policies. The apology was a significant step toward reconciliation and marked a turning point in the nation's efforts to heal historical wounds.

The apology was received with mixed emotions by those directly affected by the policies. For some, it provided a sense of acknowledgment and closure, while for others, the pain of the past remains deeply ingrained.

In conclusion, the chapter on the Stolen Generations and Apology is a poignant reminder of the atrocities committed against Indigenous Australians in the pursuit of misguided assimilation policies. It highlights the resilience and strength of Indigenous communities and their ongoing journey toward healing and reconciliation. The apology, though a powerful moment in history, cannot undo the past but serves as a crucial step in acknowledging the truth and working towards a more just and equitable future for all Australians.

Australian Politics and Government

The political landscape of Australia is a dynamic and intricate web of institutions, practices, and traditions that have evolved over centuries. As a democratic nation, Australia's political system is built on a foundation of British parliamentary democracy, but it has also developed its unique characteristics and features. This chapter delves into the essential elements of Australian politics and government, providing insight into how the nation is governed.

Constitutional Monarchy: Australia is a constitutional monarchy, with a reigning monarch as the head of state. However, the monarch's powers are largely ceremonial, and the day-to-day governance of the country is carried out by elected officials.

Federal System: Australia is a federation comprising six states and two territories. Each state and territory has its government with a range of powers, while the federal government is responsible for matters that affect the nation as a whole, such as defense and foreign affairs.

Parliamentary Democracy: Australia's political system is characterized by a parliamentary democracy. This means that the government is formed by the political party or coalition with the majority of seats in the House of Representatives, the lower house of the federal parliament.

Bicameral Parliament: The federal parliament consists of two houses—the House of Representatives and the Senate. The House of Representatives is made up of members elected from individual electoral divisions, while the Senate has equal representation from each state and territory, with members known as senators.

Prime Minister: The leader of the political party or coalition that holds the majority in the House of Representatives becomes the Prime Minister. The Prime Minister is the head of government and is responsible for the administration of the country.

Cabinet: The Cabinet is composed of senior government ministers chosen by the Prime Minister. They are responsible for making important policy decisions and implementing government initiatives.

Governor-General: As the representative of the monarch in Australia, the Governor-General performs various ceremonial duties and plays a crucial constitutional role. The Governor-General grants royal assent to bills passed by parliament, which is the final step in the legislative process.

Elections: Federal elections are held to choose members of the House of Representatives and the Senate. State and territory elections are also held separately. Voting in federal elections is compulsory for eligible Australian citizens.

Political Parties: Australia has a multi-party system, with the two major parties being the Australian Labor Party (ALP) and the Liberal Party of Australia. Other significant parties include the National Party, the Australian Greens, and various minor parties and independents.

Preferential Voting: Australia uses a preferential voting system, where voters rank candidates in order of preference. This system aims to ensure that elected representatives have broad support from their constituents.

Compulsory Voting: Australian citizens are required by law to enroll and vote in federal elections once they reach the age of 18. Failure to vote without a valid reason can result in fines.

Referendums: Changes to the Australian Constitution require a referendum, which is a nationwide vote. Referendums are relatively rare and often focus on significant constitutional amendments.

Public Service: Australia has a professional public service that provides advice and supports the government in implementing policies and programs. The public service operates independently and impartially.

Independent Judiciary: The Australian legal system is independent of the government, with judges appointed based on merit and serving for life or until retirement. The judiciary plays a critical role in interpreting and upholding the law.

In summary, Australian politics and government are characterized by a blend of democratic principles, British parliamentary traditions, and a commitment to the rule of law. The nation's political system is designed to ensure accountability, representation, and the protection of individual rights. While the political landscape may be subject to change and evolution, these fundamental principles remain at the core of Australia's democratic governance.

Economy and Trade Down Under

Australia's economy is a robust and diverse powerhouse, characterized by its stability, abundant natural resources, and strong trade ties with the world. In this chapter, we will explore the key aspects of Australia's economy, its major industries, trade partners, and the factors that contribute to its economic prosperity.

Economic Stability: Australia is renowned for its economic stability, which is a result of prudent fiscal policies, a well-regulated financial sector, and political stability. The nation has experienced uninterrupted economic growth for over two decades.

Natural Resources: One of Australia's primary strengths lies in its vast natural resources. The country is a leading exporter of minerals, including iron ore, coal, gold, and natural gas. These resources have played a pivotal role in fueling the nation's economic growth.

Agriculture: Agriculture is a significant contributor to the Australian economy. The country is known for its agricultural exports, including wheat, beef, dairy products, and wool. Advanced farming practices and technology have enabled Australia to be a global agricultural powerhouse.

Services Sector: The services sector is a major driver of the Australian economy, encompassing industries such as finance, healthcare, education, and tourism. Australia's well-developed education and healthcare systems contribute to its reputation as a high-quality service provider.

Mining and Resources: The mining industry is a cornerstone of Australia's economy. It not only provides substantial revenue through exports but also supports related industries and infrastructure development. Australia is a key global player in the extraction of resources.

Trade Partners: Australia's geographical location in the Asia-Pacific region has led to strong trade relationships with neighboring countries. China, Japan, and South Korea are among its top trading partners. The Australia-United States Free Trade Agreement (AUSFTA) is also significant in fostering trade with the United States.

Exports and Imports: The country's exports include minerals, agricultural products, education services, and manufactured goods. Imports consist of machinery, vehicles, electronics, and petroleum products. Australia's trade balance has been positive for many years.

Investment: Australia attracts foreign investment across various sectors due to its stable economy and strong legal framework. Foreign direct investment plays a crucial role in the nation's economic growth.

Innovation and Research: Australia invests in innovation and research, with a focus on cutting-edge technologies, medical research, and renewable energy. Research institutions and universities collaborate with industries to drive innovation.

Challenges: Like any economy, Australia faces challenges, including the need to diversify beyond resources, environmental sustainability, and addressing income inequality.

Government Role: The Australian government plays a pivotal role in shaping economic policies, ensuring regulatory frameworks are conducive to business, and fostering trade relationships globally.

Economic Resilience: Australia's economic resilience was evident during the global financial crisis when it weathered the storm better than many other nations, a testament to its strong economic fundamentals.

In conclusion, Australia's economy and trade are vibrant and multifaceted. The nation's ability to adapt to changing global economic dynamics, coupled with its commitment to innovation and sustainability, positions it as a significant player in the global economy. Australia's economic story is one of resilience, diversification, and a commitment to excellence on the world stage.

Australian Innovation and Technology

Australia's commitment to innovation and technology has positioned it as a global player in various cutting-edge industries. In this chapter, we will explore the nation's strides in innovation, technological advancements, and the sectors where Australia has made a significant impact.

Research and Development: Australia invests heavily in research and development (R&D), with a focus on areas such as medical research, renewable energy, and information technology. Leading research institutions and universities collaborate with industries to drive innovation.

Medical Breakthroughs: Australia is known for its contributions to medical research and healthcare innovations. Notable achievements include the development of the Gardasil vaccine for cervical cancer and advancements in organ transplant procedures.

Renewable Energy: With its abundant sunshine and wind resources, Australia has embraced renewable energy technologies. The country is a leader in solar and wind energy production and has made substantial investments in clean energy projects.

Space Exploration: Australia is actively involved in space exploration and satellite technology. It hosts various ground stations for tracking and communicating with spacecraft contributing to global space initiatives.

Information Technology: The Australian IT sector has grown significantly, with thriving start-up ecosystems in cities like Sydney and Melbourne. The country has a strong focus on cybersecurity, data analytics, and artificial intelligence.

Biotechnology: Australia's biotechnology industry is flourishing, with innovations in genetic research, pharmaceuticals, and biopharmaceutical manufacturing.

Education and Training: The Australian government promotes STEM (Science, Technology, Engineering, and Mathematics) education, producing a skilled workforce that fuels the technology sector's growth.

Innovation Hubs: Innovation hubs and tech precincts have emerged in various cities, fostering collaboration between start-ups, established companies, and research institutions.

Start-up Ecosystem: Australia's start-up ecosystem is vibrant, supported by government initiatives and venture capital funding. These start-ups often focus on emerging technologies and innovative solutions.

Cybersecurity: Australia places a strong emphasis on cybersecurity, recognizing its importance in safeguarding critical infrastructure and data. The government has implemented cybersecurity strategies to protect against cyber threats.

Telecommunications: Australia has a modern telecommunications infrastructure, including the rollout of the National Broadband Network (NBN), which aims to provide high-speed internet access to homes and businesses across the country.

Innovative Agriculture: The agriculture sector benefits from technology adoption, with innovations in precision agriculture, sustainable farming practices, and the use of data-driven solutions to optimize crop yields.

Collaboration with Global Partners: Australia collaborates with international partners on various research projects, space exploration, and scientific endeavors, contributing to global advancements.

Challenges: While Australia has made significant strides in innovation and technology, challenges such as digital inclusion, the digital divide in rural areas, and cybersecurity threats require ongoing attention.

In summary, Australia's commitment to innovation and technology has placed it at the forefront of global advancements in various sectors. The nation's investment in research, its skilled workforce, and its collaborative approach with international partners continue to drive progress and shape the future of technology. Australia's innovation journey is marked by a pioneering spirit that seeks to tackle complex challenges and create a brighter, technologically-driven future.

Australian Film and Television

Australia has a rich and vibrant film and television industry that has made a significant impact both domestically and on the global stage. In this chapter, we will delve into the history, achievements, and notable figures that have shaped the country's cinematic and television landscape.

Early Beginnings: Australian cinema dates back to the late 19th century when pioneers like the Tait brothers produced the first Australian feature film, "The Story of the Kelly Gang," in 1906. This marked the beginning of a unique cinematic journey.

Golden Age of Australian Cinema: The 1970s and 1980s are often referred to as the golden age of Australian cinema. Filmmakers like Peter Weir, George Miller, and Fred Schepisi gained international recognition for their works, including "Picnic at Hanging Rock," "Mad Max," and "The Chant of Jimmie Blacksmith."

Awards and Accolades: Australian films have received acclaim at major international film festivals and awards ceremonies. "The Piano," directed by Jane Campion, won the Palme d'Or at the Cannes Film Festival in 1993, and "Shine" earned Geoffrey Rush an Academy Award for Best Actor in 1996.

Distinctive Australian Stories: Australian cinema often explores unique cultural and social themes, reflecting the nation's diverse identity. Films like "Rabbit-Proof Fence" and "Samson and Delilah" address Indigenous issues, while

"The Castle" offers a satirical take on Australian suburban life.

Global Success: Australian actors and actresses have made their mark on the international stage. Notable figures include Cate Blanchett, Nicole Kidman, Hugh Jackman, and Russell Crowe, who have achieved critical acclaim and worldwide recognition.

Television Industry: Australia has a thriving television industry that produces a wide range of content, from drama series like "Neighbours" and "Home and Away" to iconic shows like "Skippy the Bush Kangaroo." The Australian Broadcasting Corporation (ABC) and commercial networks like Channel Seven and Channel Nine play significant roles in television production.

Cultural Impact: Television has been a powerful medium for reflecting Australian culture and society. Shows like "Kath & Kim" and "The Sullivans" have left a lasting cultural impact and are beloved by Australian audiences.

International Collaborations: Australian filmmakers and actors frequently collaborate with international productions, contributing to the global entertainment industry. The success of Australian talent in Hollywood underscores the country's influence in film and television.

Supporting Indigenous Voices: Australia's film and television industry is increasingly focused on supporting Indigenous voices and stories. Films like "Sweet Country" and "The Sapphires" shed light on Indigenous experiences and heritage.

Challenges and Opportunities: The industry faces challenges such as funding limitations and competition from international content. However, opportunities for growth and innovation continue to arise, driven by digital streaming platforms and evolving viewer preferences.

In conclusion, Australian film and television have made indelible marks on the world stage, showcasing distinctive stories, talent, and creativity. The industry's commitment to diversity, unique storytelling, and collaboration with global partners ensures that it will remain a vital and influential part of Australia's cultural landscape. From classic films to contemporary series, Australian entertainment continues to captivate audiences both at home and abroad.

Literature and Authors from the Land Down Under

Australia has a rich literary tradition that reflects the nation's diverse cultural heritage and unique landscapes. In this chapter, we will explore the history of Australian literature and some of the most renowned authors who have emerged from the Land Down Under.

Early Beginnings: Australian literature has its roots in the storytelling traditions of Indigenous peoples, who have passed down oral histories for thousands of years. These stories, often referred to as Dreamtime or Dreaming stories, are integral to the Indigenous cultural identity.

Colonial Literature: The arrival of European settlers in the late 18th century marked the beginning of written literature in Australia. Early colonial writers, such as Henry Lawson and Banjo Paterson, captured the harshness of the Australian bush and the struggles of pioneering life in their works.

Banjo Paterson: A.B. "Banjo" Paterson is one of Australia's most celebrated poets and authors. His iconic poem "Waltzing Matilda" has become a national anthem of sorts, and his bush ballads, including "The Man from Snowy River," continue to resonate with readers.

Henry Lawson: Henry Lawson, another prominent figure in Australian literature, wrote about the lives of ordinary Australians in the bush and urban settings. His short stories and poems, such as "The Drover's Wife" and "The Loaded

Dog," capture the essence of Australian life in the late 19th and early 20th centuries.

Modern Australian Literature: In the 20th century, Australian literature underwent significant transformations. Authors like Patrick White, who won the Nobel Prize in Literature in 1973, explored themes of identity and culture in their works. White's novel "Voss" is considered a masterpiece of Australian literature.

Tim Winton: Tim Winton is known for his novels set in the rugged landscapes of Western Australia. His works, including "Cloudstreet" and "Breath," are characterized by their vivid descriptions of the natural environment and their exploration of the human condition.

Contemporary Voices: Contemporary Australian literature is marked by diverse voices and genres. Authors like Kate Grenville, Markus Zusak, and Liane Moriarty have gained international recognition for their novels, spanning historical fiction, young adult literature, and contemporary fiction.

Indigenous Literature: Indigenous Australian authors, such as Alexis Wright and Tara June Winch, have made significant contributions to the literary world. Their works often draw on Indigenous storytelling traditions and address themes of identity, history, and cultural preservation.

Booker Prize Winners: Australian authors have also received prestigious literary awards, with Richard Flanagan winning the Man Booker Prize in 2014 for his novel "The Narrow Road to the Deep North."

Publishing Industry: Australia has a thriving publishing industry, with numerous publishing houses producing a wide range of literature. Literary festivals, such as the Sydney Writers' Festival and the Melbourne Writers Festival, celebrate the written word and provide a platform for authors to engage with readers.

Global Impact: Australian literature has a global reach, with many authors' works translated into multiple languages. It continues to engage with themes of identity, multiculturalism, and the ever-evolving Australian experience.

In conclusion, Australian literature reflects the nation's history, culture, and the diverse voices that have emerged from this vast and unique land. From the Dreamtime stories of Indigenous Australians to the contemporary novels of modern authors, Australian literature offers a rich tapestry of storytelling that resonates both locally and internationally. It is a testament to the enduring power of words to capture the essence of a nation and its people.

Adventure and Outdoor Activities

Australia, with its diverse landscapes and stunning natural beauty, offers a wide range of adventure and outdoor activities for enthusiasts of all kinds. From the rugged Outback to the pristine coastline, this chapter explores the thrilling experiences awaiting those who seek adventure in the Land Down Under.

Hiking and Bushwalking: Australia boasts an extensive network of hiking trails that cater to all levels of experience. The Great Ocean Walk in Victoria offers breathtaking coastal views, while the Larapinta Trail in the Northern Territory takes you through the heart of the Outback. The iconic Overland Track in Tasmania provides a challenging trek through ancient rainforests and alpine landscapes.

Camping: Camping is a popular pastime in Australia, and there are countless campgrounds situated in some of the most picturesque locations. Whether you prefer beachside camping along the Great Barrier Reef or remote camping in the Flinders Ranges, there's a camping experience to suit your preferences.

Rock Climbing: For rock climbing enthusiasts, the Grampians in Victoria and the Blue Mountains in New South Wales offer world-class climbing opportunities. These stunning natural formations provide a challenging and rewarding experience for climbers of all levels.

Surfing: Australia is renowned for its surf culture and world-class waves. The Gold Coast in Queensland, Bells

Beach in Victoria, and Margaret River in Western Australia are just a few of the iconic surf spots. Whether you're a seasoned surfer or a beginner looking to catch your first wave, there's a spot for you.

Scuba Diving: The Great Barrier Reef, the world's largest coral reef system, is a mecca for scuba divers. Explore the vibrant underwater world and encounter a dazzling array of marine life, including colorful corals, sharks, and turtles. The reef's crystal-clear waters make it a paradise for divers.

Snorkeling: If you prefer to stay near the water's surface, snorkeling is an excellent way to experience the Great Barrier Reef's wonders. The Whitsunday Islands and the Ningaloo Reef in Western Australia also offer exceptional snorkeling opportunities.

Sailing: Australia's extensive coastline makes it a prime destination for sailing enthusiasts. The Whitsundays, in particular, are a sailor's paradise, with their calm waters and idyllic islands. Join a sailing tour or charter your own vessel to explore this stunning region.

White-Water Rafting: The wild rivers of Tasmania, Victoria, and Queensland provide thrilling white-water rafting adventures. Tackle challenging rapids and navigate pristine waterways while surrounded by breathtaking natural beauty.

Skydiving: For the ultimate adrenaline rush, take to the skies with a tandem skydiving experience. Imagine free-falling over iconic landmarks like the Sydney Harbour or the Great Ocean Road.

Hot Air Ballooning: Experience the serenity of floating above the Australian landscape in a hot air balloon. The Yarra Valley in Victoria and the Atherton Tablelands in Queensland offer unforgettable ballooning experiences.

4WD Adventures: The Australian Outback is a playground for off-road enthusiasts. Embark on 4WD adventures to explore remote and rugged landscapes, including the famous Simpson Desert and the Kimberley region.

Wildlife Encounters: Australia's unique wildlife is a draw for nature lovers. Take guided tours to see kangaroos, koalas, and other native species in their natural habitats.

Abseiling and Caving: For those who enjoy descending into the depths, Australia's caves and limestone formations provide exciting abseiling and caving opportunities.

Mountain Biking: The mountain biking trails in Australia cater to riders of all skill levels. From the purpose-built trails in the Blue Derby in Tasmania to the scenic routes in the Snowy Mountains, there's a trail for every cyclist.

In Australia, adventure and outdoor activities are not just pastimes; they are a way of life. Whether you're seeking heart-pounding thrills or peaceful moments in nature, this vast and diverse country offers an abundance of opportunities to satisfy your adventurous spirit. So, gear up and get ready to explore the wonders of the Australian wilderness, where every day is an opportunity for a new and exhilarating experience.

Planning Your Trip to Australia

Planning a trip to Australia is an exciting endeavor, as it offers a diverse range of experiences and attractions for travelers. Whether you're an adventure enthusiast, a nature lover, or a culture seeker, Australia has something to offer everyone. Here, we'll guide you through the essential aspects of planning your trip to this remarkable destination.

1. Visa and Entry Requirements: Before booking your flight, ensure you have the necessary visa to enter Australia. Most tourists will require either a Visitor Visa (subclass 600) or an Electronic Travel Authority (ETA) depending on their nationality. The application process is straightforward and can usually be done online.

2. Best Time to Visit: Australia's vast size means that its climate varies from region to region. The best time to visit depends on your preferences and the activities you plan to do. Generally, the summer months (December to February) are ideal for beachgoers, while the spring (September to November) and autumn (March to May) offer pleasant weather for outdoor activities. Winter (June to August) is perfect for exploring the southern regions and enjoying snow sports.

3. Duration of Stay: Determine how long you intend to stay in Australia, as this will influence your itinerary. Australia is vast, and it's impossible to see everything in one trip. Consider focusing on specific regions or cities to make the most of your visit.

4. Accommodation: Australia offers a wide range of accommodation options, from luxury hotels to budget hostels and unique stays like glamping and eco lodges. Book your accommodation well in advance, especially during peak tourist seasons.

5. Flights: Research and compare flights to find the best deals. Major cities like Sydney, Melbourne, Brisbane, and Perth are well-connected internationally. Consider using flight comparison websites to find affordable options.

6. Travel Insurance: It's essential to have comprehensive travel insurance that covers unexpected events like medical emergencies, trip cancellations, and lost luggage. Check the policy to ensure it suits your needs.

7. Currency: Australia's currency is the Australian Dollar (AUD). Familiarize yourself with currency exchange rates and be prepared to use both cash and cards for transactions.

8. Vaccinations: While Australia is generally a safe destination health-wise, it's a good idea to consult your healthcare provider for any recommended vaccinations or health precautions before your trip.

9. Itinerary: Plan a rough itinerary, considering the places you want to visit and the experiences you want to have. Australia offers a diverse range of attractions, from iconic landmarks to hidden gems in remote areas.

10. Transportation: Australia's extensive road network makes road trips a popular option. Renting a car or campervan can provide flexibility in exploring the country. Public transportation is also readily available in major cities.

11. Activities and Tours: Research and book any activities or tours you'd like to participate in ahead of time. This can include guided wildlife encounters, diving excursions, or cultural experiences.

12. Language: English is the official language in Australia. While most Australians speak English, you may encounter various accents and local slang. Familiarize yourself with common Australian phrases to enhance your communication.

13. Travel Documents: Ensure you have all your essential travel documents, including your passport, visa, travel insurance details, flight tickets, and accommodation reservations, organized in one place.

14. Safety: Australia is known for its safety, but it's still important to take standard precautions like safeguarding your belongings, following local advice, and being aware of your surroundings.

15. Respect Local Customs: Familiarize yourself with Australian customs and etiquette. Australians are generally friendly and welcoming, and showing respect for their culture will enhance your experience.

Planning a trip to Australia requires careful consideration and preparation, but the rewards are boundless. From the vibrant cities to the stunning natural wonders, Australia offers a wealth of experiences for every traveler. With thorough planning, you can make the most of your visit to this extraordinary country and create memories that will last a lifetime.

Must-See Tourist Sights in Australia

Australia is a land of breathtaking natural beauty, iconic landmarks, and cultural treasures that captivate travelers from around the world. In this chapter, we'll explore some of the must-see tourist sights that you should include in your Australian adventure. These iconic destinations showcase the diversity and splendor of this vast continent.

1. Sydney Opera House: One of the world's most recognized architectural masterpieces, the Sydney Opera House graces the shores of Sydney Harbour. Its unique design and stunning location make it a must-see for visitors. Attend a performance or simply admire the building from the outside.

2. Sydney Harbour Bridge: Known as the "Coathanger" due to its distinctive shape, the Sydney Harbour Bridge offers panoramic views of the city. You can climb the bridge for a thrilling experience or stroll across it at your leisure.

3. Uluru (Ayers Rock): Located in the heart of the Australian Outback, Uluru is a sacred site for indigenous Australians and a UNESCO World Heritage-listed wonder. Witness the dramatic color changes of this massive sandstone monolith at sunrise or sunset.

4. Great Barrier Reef: The world's largest coral reef system, the Great Barrier Reef is a paradise for divers and snorkelers. Explore its vibrant underwater world, teeming with marine life, or take a scenic flight to admire its beauty from above.

5. The Twelve Apostles: Along the Great Ocean Road in Victoria, you'll find the Twelve Apostles, a collection of limestone stacks rising majestically from the Southern Ocean. Witness their dramatic beauty against the backdrop of the cliffs.

6. Great Ocean Road: This coastal drive is an attraction in itself, winding along breathtaking cliffs, lush rainforests, and pristine beaches. Stop at lookouts and coastal towns for a taste of Australian coastal life.

7. Kakadu National Park: Located in the Northern Territory, Kakadu is Australia's largest national park and a UNESCO World Heritage site. It's home to diverse ecosystems, ancient Aboriginal rock art, and abundant wildlife.

8. Bondi Beach: A symbol of Australian beach culture, Bondi Beach in Sydney is a great place to relax, swim, surf, or simply soak up the sun. It's a popular spot for both locals and tourists.

9. The Daintree Rainforest: This ancient rainforest in Queensland is a living testament to Australia's unique biodiversity. Take a guided tour to explore its lush greenery, spot wildlife, and learn about its ecological significance.

10. The Whitsunday Islands: With their pristine white-sand beaches and crystal-clear waters, the Whitsundays are a tropical paradise. Sailing, snorkeling, and exploring the Great Barrier Reef are popular activities here.

11. Melbourne's Laneways: Melbourne is known for its vibrant street art and hidden laneways filled with cafes, boutiques, and art galleries. Exploring these laneways is a must for experiencing the city's creative culture.

12. The Royal Botanic Garden, Sydney: This beautifully landscaped garden is a peaceful oasis in the heart of Sydney. Stroll through its lush gardens, visit the iconic Mrs. Macquarie's Chair, and enjoy stunning views of the harbor.

13. The Pinnacles Desert: Located in Nambung National Park, Western Australia, the Pinnacles Desert features thousands of limestone pillars rising from the desert floor. It's a surreal and otherworldly landscape.

14. The Australian War Memorial: Located in Canberra, the capital city, this memorial pays tribute to Australia's military history. It's a place of reflection and honor, with informative exhibits and a moving Last Post ceremony.

15. The Tarkine Wilderness: In Tasmania, the Tarkine Wilderness offers pristine landscapes of forests, rivers, and rugged coastline. It's a haven for nature lovers and hikers.

These are just a few of the must-see tourist sights in Australia. Each of these destinations offers a unique and unforgettable experience, showcasing the remarkable beauty and cultural richness of this extraordinary country. Whether you're drawn to natural wonders, urban adventures, or indigenous heritage, Australia has something to enchant every traveler.

Epilogue

As we reach the end of this journey through the land Down Under, it's worth reflecting on the diverse and captivating tapestry that is Australia. From its ancient indigenous history to its modern multicultural society, from the vast, untamed outback to the bustling cities on the coast, Australia offers a wealth of experiences for those who seek to explore it.

Throughout this book, we've delved into the rich history of this continent, starting with the indigenous peoples who have called it home for over 65,000 years. We've traced the footsteps of early European explorers who navigated its shores, the arrival of the First Fleet and the establishment of convict settlements, and the dramatic changes brought about by colonization and the Gold Rush.

We've explored the birth of the Australian nation through Federation, its role in the World Wars, and its transformation into a modern, multicultural society. We've marveled at the unique geography and climate, including the world-famous Great Barrier Reef and the rugged Australian Outback. We've delved into the diverse wildlife that inhabits this land, from kangaroos and koalas to crocodiles and colorful birdlife.

We've savored the flavors of Australian cuisine, from Vegemite to Tim Tams, and learned about iconic dishes and beverages that define the country's culinary identity We've visited its most important cities, such as Sydney Melbourne, and Brisbane, each with its own distinct character and cultural offerings.

We've explored the deep-rooted cultural aspects, including indigenous Dreamtime stories, modern Australian art and music, and the passion for sports like cricket and rugby. We've uncovered the unique language and slang that Australians use, creating a dialect that's both familiar and distinctive.

We've delved into the country's vibrant festivals and celebrations, its customs and etiquette, and its education and healthcare systems. We've examined its commitment to environmental conservation and the efforts to protect its natural treasures. We've also discussed the important issues of indigenous rights and reconciliation, as well as the complex history of the Stolen Generations and the formal apology made to them.

We've gained insights into the political landscape, the economy, and Australia's role in global trade. We've celebrated its achievements in innovation and technology, and we've appreciated its contributions to the world of film, television, literature, and the arts.

Finally, we've highlighted the incredible outdoor adventures awaiting those who venture to Australia, from exploring the rugged landscapes to partaking in thrilling activities and enjoying the pristine beaches.

Australia is a land of contrasts and contradictions, a place where ancient traditions meet modern progress, and where natural beauty is both breathtaking and rugged. It's a nation that cherishes its past while embracing its future, and it welcomes travelers with open arms to experience its wonders.

As you consider planning your own journey to Australia, remember that this vast and diverse country has so much more to offer than can be covered in a single book. Its beauty and complexity are best appreciated in person, as you immerse yourself in its landscapes, culture, and people.

So, whether you're drawn to the iconic sights, the rich history, the unique wildlife, or the warm and welcoming locals, know that Australia awaits your exploration with open skies and boundless horizons. May your journey be filled with unforgettable moments and treasured memories.

Thank you for joining me on this voyage through the Land Down Under.

Printed in Great Britain
by Amazon